SNOWCAPS
ON THE EQUATOR

Nyiragongo from Nyamlagira's shattered Kitazungurwa Ridge, torn apart in July 1986, when a new volcanic vent exploded into being.

SNOWCAPS
ON THE EQUATOR

*The Fabled Mountains of Kenya,
Tanzania, Uganda and Zaire*

Photographs by Clive Ward
Written by Gordon Boy and Iain Allan

THE BODLEY HEAD
LONDON

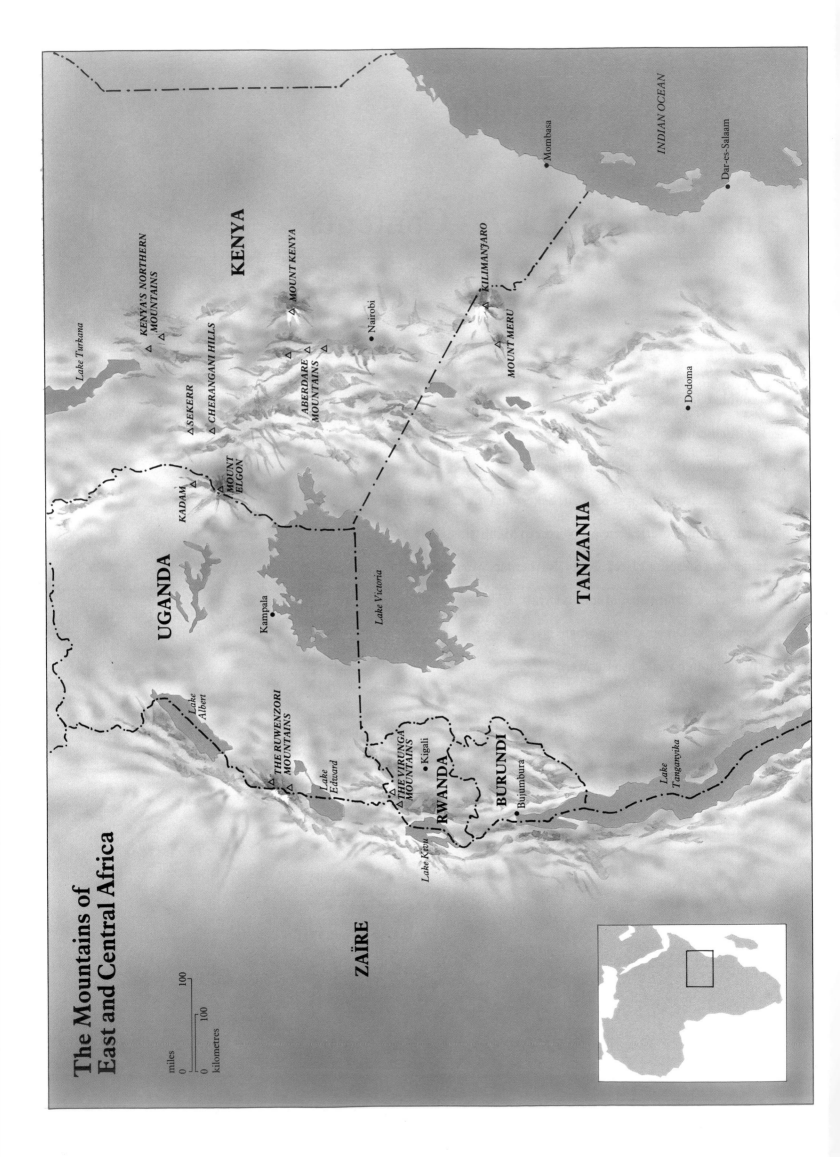

The Mountains of East and Central Africa

miles
0
100

kilometres
0
100

INDIAN OCEAN

• Mombasa

Dar-es-Salaam •

KENYA

KENYA'S NORTHERN MOUNTAINS △
△

△ MOUNT KENYA

△ KILIMANJARO

Lake Turkana

△ SEKERR
△ CHERANGANI HILLS

△
△ ABERDARE MOUNTAINS

• Nairobi

△ MOUNT MERU

Dodoma •

△ KADAM
△ MOUNT ELGON

UGANDA

TANZANIA

Lake Victoria

• Kampala

Lake Albert

THE RUWENZORI MOUNTAINS
△ △

Lake Edward

△ THE VIRUNGA MOUNTAINS
• Kigali

BURUNDI

Lake Tanganyika

ZAÏRE

RWANDA

Lake Kivu

• Bujumbura

Introduction

Over the years our climbing and walking in East and Central Africa have given us a personal acquaintance with its mountains, yet we are very aware that each of us can know only a small fraction of what is there. *Snowcaps on the Equator* aims to document and interpret visual and selected experiences. These are the personal experiences of others and of ourselves, and therefore are often unique.

During our travels we have become aware of changes within the mountains. Glaciers are receding, while some areas become wetter, others drier. There are conflicting views within the spectrum of expert opinion on environmental matters, but whatever the view may be, there is no getting away from the fact that there is change. Our intention is to play our own small part and "freeze" the mountains in the present moment through our description of them.

It has been impossible to cover every volcano and hill range scattered around East and Central Africa. We have had to wrestle with the problem not of what to put in, but rather what to leave out. Many of the mountains that we have included are little known, and because of this they have their own charm. Their summits are magnificent, covered in hardwoods, cycads, mosses and delicate flowers, stepping stones to Equatorial Africa's snow and ice.

Africa's mountains are imbued with legends and mysteries. We felt it necessary to elaborate on some of these. Early man had his links with the mountains; their springs, rocks and summits were for him the dwelling places of venerated spirits.

Nineteenth-century explorers, perhaps unknowingly drawn back to their origins, made it known to the outside world that in the "Dark Continent" there existed worthy challenges for climbers on mountains far higher than those in Europe. Settlers followed and kindred spirits formed mountain clubs. Many of these climbers used African mountains as a springboard, and went on to achieve great climbing feats in the Himalayas and the Andes.

Snowcaps on the Equator will, we hope, open up these peaks for those who seek remote mountain areas where the scope is boundless for the adventure-seeker. Even with Kilimanjaro, which has one of the most trodden summits in Africa, two-thirds of the Alpine zone is seldom visited.

Africa is a lodestone. Its mountains are charismatic, its mountain ecosystem, peaks and climbing routes, are all unique. They form a magic circle from which it is difficult to break at will. Once touched, these mountains are not something you can leave for ever and not return to . . . We wish you a fruitful odyssey.

Clive Ward
Gordon Boy
Iain Allan

Nairobi, February 1988

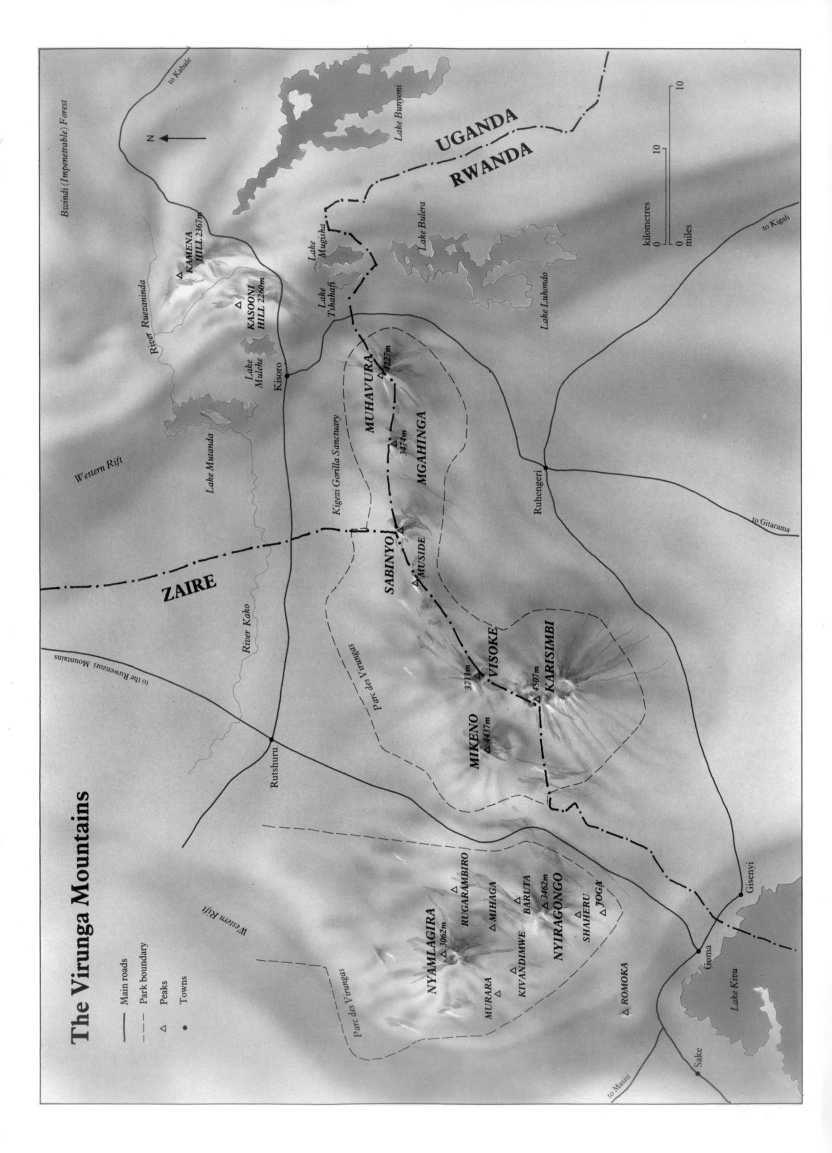

The Virunga Mountains

Main roads
Park boundary
△ Peaks
• Towns

N

UGANDA
RWANDA

ZAIRE

Bwindi (Impenetrable Forest)

to Kabale

to Kigali

to Gitarama

kilometres
miles
10
10
0
0

KAMENA
HILL 2367m △

KASOONI
HILL 2260m △

River Ruezaminda

Lake Bunyomi

Lake Mugisha

Lake Tshahafi

Lake Bulera

Lake Luhondo

Lake Mulehe

Kisoro

Lake Mutanda

Western Rift

Kigezi Gorilla Sanctuary

Ruhengeri

MUHAVURA
△ 4227m

MGAHINGA
△ 3474m

SABINYO
△
MUSIDE
3711m △

VISOKE

KARISIMBI
△ 4507m

MIKENO
△ 4437m

Parc des Virungas

River Kako

to the Ruwenzori Mountains

Rutshuru

Western Rift

Parc des Virungas

NYAMLAGIRA
△ 3062m

RUGARAMBIRO △

△ MIHAGA

MURARA △

△ KIVANDIMWE

BARUTA
△ 3462m

NYIRAGONGO

SHAHERU
△

△ JOGA

△ ROMOKA

Gisenyi

Goma

Lake Kivu

Sake

to Masisi

1 · Troubled Spirits: The Virunga Mountains

Gordon Boy

A chain of eight towering volcanoes, the Virunga Mountains straddle the convergent frontiers of Rwanda, Zaïre and Uganda. Their lofty cones, disposed east-west across the breadth of the volatile Western Rift, dominate the green heart of the Central African lake region.

Today the remote volcanoes are best known as the refuge place of one of only two remaining colonies of mountain gorillas (*Gorilla gorilla berengei*). The beleaguered colony, now down to just 280 animals, is thought to represent nearly three-quarters of the world's entire population of this endangered primate subspecies.

The two most westerly volcanoes, 3,062-m (10,046-ft) Mount Nyamlagira and 3,462-m (11,358-ft) Mount Nyiragongo, are both still highly active. Both mountains have for much of this century been spitting fire from parasitic cones and fissures on their slopes. Four new vents have burst into activity since 1980, sending red-hot flows of lava hurtling down the valleys.

The Kitazungurwa fissure, low down near the southern foot of Nyamlagira, was the site of the latest upheaval. The night of July 16, 1986 saw it explode into being, amid a burst of showering ash. Blazing lava, thrust up in a surging fountain, lit up the night sky. Glowing debris oozed down from the gaping vent.

Puffs of steam, infused with choking sulphur fumes, still rise from Kitazungurwa's ash-pit. Inside, in cracks in the black lava crust, molten rock, glowing red, still smoulders ominously. Brittle lava bombs, strewn far across the shattered hillside, betray the force of the initial blast.

From the nearby Kivandimwe vent Nyamlagira unleashed similar outpourings in both 1981 and 1984. And on December 31, 1981 there was a spectacular New Year's Eve explosion of fireworks from the Rugarambiro fissure, high up on the saddle between Nyamlagira and Nyiragongo.

Burning up forest and farmland alike, the Rugarambiro lava flows blazed a trail of devastation that was to extend for nearly six kilometres (four miles) down the wide Rutshuru Valley, to the east. Bukumu, a small village nestled in the valley, had to be evacuated.

The last eruption with fatal consequences for people living in the region was in January 1977. A small, bubbling lava pool which had been smouldering away for more than half a century in the deep pit of Nyiragongo's summit crater welled up, suddenly, into a brimming, incandescent lake. The overflow, spewing out through the volcano's high-lying Baruta, Shaheru and Djoga side-fissures, tore down the mountainside at speeds of up to 60 km/h (approximately 35 mph), fanning out in broad, metre-thick torrents which incinerated all that lay before them.

Not heralded by the usual preliminary earth tremors, the fiery avalanche caught the Banyaruanda peasant-farming community at the foot of the volcano

Lava bomb on scarred hillside near the Kitazungurwa fissure on Nyamlagira, far eastern Zaïre.

completely unawares. Seventy people were burned alive, and a further 800 left homeless. More than 1,200 hectares (approximately 3,000 acres) of farmland were laid waste. The eruption lasted barely seven hours.

That such upheavals have been wreaking havoc in the area for centuries is borne out by the myths of the Bahutu, the most populous of the region's three Banyaruanda peoples. Of Bantu stock, the Bahutu have been tilling the fertile Virunga foothills since about the eighth century AD. For them the eight lofty volcanoes are the mystical abode of the souls of departed tribal ancestors. In consequence, the frequent eruptions have far more than just physical repercussions for them. Bahutu mythology is rife with tales of violent outbursts by aggrieved and vengeful spirits. Still, lament wary local farmers, these troubled spirits will not sleep.

In Kinyaruanda, the language spoken by the Bahutu and by the region's two minority Banyaruanda groups the Batwa and the Batutsi, "Virunga" (or "Birunga" as it is frequently pronounced) is the name commonly applied to all volcanic cones. Its meaning has been rendered, variously, as "that which cooks", "cooking pots" and "place where there is fire". A similar array of meanings has been assigned to "Mufumbiro" (or "Bufumbiro"), the name given to the mountain chain by the neighbouring Bakiga land-tillers of south-western Uganda.

Six dormant volcanoes, all of them taller than Nyamlagira and Nyiragongo, form the main body of the 70-km-long (approximately 40-mile-long) barrier of the Virunga, or Mufumbiro, chain. The loftiest, Mount Karisimbi, rises 4,507 m (14,788 ft) above sea level. Africa's sixth highest mountain, it is dwarfed only by Kilimanjaro, Mount Kenya, the Ruwenzori Mountains, the Semien Range in Ethiopia, and Tanzania's Mount Meru.

A huge dome of a mountain, Karisimbi dominates the central portion of the

(*Opposite*) Debris from Zaïre's 1981 Rugarambiro eruption. Mikeno and Karisimbi, in the distance, mark the country's border with Rwanda.

Aftermath of the Kitazungurwa blast. Stifling fumes still issue from the fissure's blackened pit, while inside, in deep cracks, oozing lava smoulders.

chain. Its name, in Kinyaruanda, means "the white shell", a reference to the glistening white mantle of hail and sleet which often decks its summit. In the north-west it is connected, via a long, forest-covered saddle, to the gaunt summit pillar of 4,437-m (14,557-ft) Mount Mikeno, second highest of the eight Virunga Mountains. A savage prospect, weather-battered Mikeno, "the barren" in Kinyaruanda, was readily dubbed "the Matterhorn of Africa" by European travellers at the turn of this century.

Another saddle, leading down off Karisimbi's daunting north-easterly slope, terminates in the smaller, more secluded dome of Mount Visoke, 3,711 m (12,175 ft) above sea level. There is, cupped in the round bowl of Visoke's summit crater, an exquisite crystal lake fed by the rains, loveliest of all the chain's many liquid-blue gems.

The Visoke–Karisimbi–Mikeno cluster of volcanoes, cut off from Nyamlagira and Nyiragongo by the wide Rutshuru Valley and, in it, the main north road from Goma on Lake Kivu, constitutes the heart of the Virunga mountain chain. It is here, in the densely forested triangle described by their three summits, that most of the world's remaining mountain gorillas reside.

Mount Sabinyo, to the east, is one of three volcanoes in the chain which border on Uganda. Its name, meaning "father with huge teeth", stems from the row of five sharp rock pinnacles that protrude from the long, curved jawbone of its summit ridge. The highest of these spiky teeth stands 3,634 m (11,923 ft) above sea level. Sabinyo's crater has with time all but eroded away. Only Mikeno, of the chain's seven other great volcanoes, has a starker, more weather-beaten crown, having long since lost all semblance of a central crater.

East of Sabinyo, over the grassy dome of 3,474-m (11,398-ft) Mount Mgahinga looms the huge dark pyramid of Mount Muhavura, easternmost of the "Mufumbiro" volcanoes. At 4,127 m (13,540 ft), Muhavura, is the third highest mountain in the chain. Its soaring bulk is such that, next to it, Mgahinga looks a mere dwarf. Not surprisingly, given its prominence as a landmark, "Muhavura" means "He who brings one back on the right path".

A small lake, set like a glassy blue eye in Muhavura's shallow crater socket, seems to transfix the sky above with its cold stare. During the seasonal rains, when the lake overflows, streaks of water can be seen streaming down the furrowed mountainside like silver, glinting tears. Mudslides, triggered by centuries of storm run-off and frost-action, have left deep gashes in Muhavura's slopes. Remote and deeply scarred, the mountain's steep flanks make for some of the most rugged, and uncompromising, hiking country on the whole of the Virunga chain.

Muhavura it was that on November 29, 1861 attracted the attention of British explorers John Hanning Speke and Captain James Grant, the first Europeans to set eyes on the Virunga Mountains. The two men were then passing through what is now the Karagwe district of north-western Tanzania, on the journey that was eventually to lead them to the "fountains of the Nile", on the northern shores of Lake Victoria.

Speke, in his *Journal of the Discovery of the Source of the Nile*, published two years later in 1863, relates how, while returning home to camp after a fruitless afternoon's hunting, his "attention was attracted by observing in the distance some bold sky-scraping cones in the country Ruanda, which at once brought back to recollection the ill-defined story I had heard from the Arabs of a wonderful hill always covered with clouds, on which snow or hail was constantly falling.

"This was a valuable discovery," he goes on to remark, "for I found these hills to be the great turn-point of the Central African watershed."

In reckoning their height to reach 10,000 ft (3,048 m), Speke conceded that the "bold sky-scraping cones" could be the highest of the fabled "Mountains of

(*Opposite*) Karisimbi from the Parc des Volcans.

the Moon". The latter, whose identity and whereabouts had been puzzling thinkers and geographers for centuries, would come to be associated, later, with the snow-clad Ruwenzori Mountains, more than 120 km (approximately 70 miles) north of the Virunga chain.

Speke was correct, though, in pronouncing the Mufumbiro cones to be the "turn-point" of the Central African watershed. For off their slopes flow tributaries of both of Africa's two greatest rivers, the Nile and the Zaïre. The towering volcanoes, spread like a barrier across the Western Rift between Lakes Kivu and Edward, lie at the heart of the Zaïre–Nile Continental Divide.

Lake Kivu, loveliest of all the sparkling Rift Valley lakes, owes its existence to the formation, here, of the lofty cones. Cradled in the south-western Virunga foothills, due south of Nyamlagira and Nyiragongo, the lake is the result of the damming up, by lava flows from the volcanoes, of the Ruzizi River, itself formerly a headstream of the Nile. The Ruzizi's waters have, in consequence, been diverted, via Lake Tanganyika, into the Zaïre River Basin. A hundred kilometres (approximately 60 miles) long and nearly half a kilometre (approximately quarter of a mile) deep, Kivu has the distinction of being the world's gassiest large lake. Lava flows, spilling down into its waters over thousands of years from hyperactive vents on Nyamlagira and Nyiragongo, have led to a build-up in the lake of more than 400 billion litres of lethal carbon dioxide.

The fizzy lake also harbours large volumes of highly flammable methane. Commercial exploitation of this gas, under way since the mid-1970s, has aroused concern among limnologists. Meddling with the lake's strange chemistry, they fear, could offset a catastrophic gas burst of the kind unleashed in 1986 by tiny Lake Nyos, in west Africa's volcanically active Cameroon highlands, which killed nearly 2,000 local villagers. Such a burst, were one ever to issue from Lake Kivu, would have far graver consequences.

Viewed from the lofty rim of Nyiragongo's summit crater, high above the northern-lakeshore town of Goma, Kivu's beauty soon dispels all notion of its darker, more threatening side, the side that makes its waters uninhabitable to crocodiles and hippos and to all but a few species of fish. A shimmering vista of blue, resplendent with long, fjord-like inlets and a sprinkling of islands, Kivu stretches as far south of Nyiragongo as the eye can see. Not visited by any European until 1894, when it was described by the German explorer Count von Götzen, Kivu was the last of Africa's great lakes to yield up its secrets to the outside world.

Von Götzen's wanderings in 1894 culminated in his becoming the first European to scale Nyiragongo, which he declared to be "fully active" at the time. The volcano's activity was first monitored closely by Colonel Hoier, who as warden of the Parc National Albert (as the Parc des Virungas, encompassing Zaïre's sector of the mountain chain, was then known) between 1931 and 1938, chalked up more than 150 separate ascents.

During this time Nyamlagira, Nyiragongo's fiery twin, was far from quiet. Its crater, like that on Nyiragongo, had for many years contained a steaming lake of lava. On the afternoon of January 28, 1938 the indefatigable Colonel Hoier was actually at the crater's edge when, amid violent earth tremors, the volcano's central ash-cone collapsed. Nyamlagira's scalding lake, welling up before him, spilled out through a breach in the crater's western rim.

For years afterwards the crests of the two live volcanoes, lit up by the red glow of their steaming cauldrons, flickered in the night sky like giant embers, discernible in the darkness from more than 50 km (30 miles) away. Pillars of fire by night, their summits, wreathed in swirling steam, were by day spectacular pillars of cloud.

Today, both craters look bleak and utterly forlorn. Barren, black lava crusts have formed where the torrid pools of fiery magma once oozed and spluttered.

Sulphurous fumes still issue, intermittently, from Nyiragongo's inner depths.

In form, Nyiragongo is a regular cone. Its slopes taper up steeply from all sides, perfectly symmetrical but for the bulging presence, north and south, of the Baruta and Shaheru parasitic cones, both almost mountains in themselves. Nyiragongo's crater, circular with a diameter of about a kilometre (five-eighths of a mile), is probably no more than 150 m (490 ft) deep.

Nyamlagira, by contrast, is a shield volcano. As such, its slopes rise only very gently from the level of the lava plain. Its base is thus very much larger than that of Nyiragongo, while its mild gradient makes it easily the most accessible and lowest-lying of the eight Virunga Mountains.

Nyamlagira's summit crater, more than six times the size of that on Nyiragongo, is comparatively very shallow. It is, however, one of only a few craters in Africa with a substantial mass of what is known as "lost land". This is land left stranded in an isolated block within a crater, "lost" because its steep sides deny all ready access. The standard text-book illustration is the "lost" island of Samosir in the lake-filled Toba caldera of northern Sumatra, in Indonesia.

On the high Virunga Mountains, generally, there is surprisingly little in the way of surface water. The soils here are thin and the lava rock soft and porous, so water from the frequent storms simply percolates into the ground instead of forming into runnels and becoming rivers. On Nyamlagira and Nyiragongo this percolating water, heated from below by the earth's boiling magma chamber, re-surfaces in the form of the numerous hot springs and steam jets on their slopes.

The great rain forests that once surrounded the Virunga Mountains have now largely made way for cultivation. The Virunga foothills, with their rich, volcanic soils, have become one of the most heavily settled rural areas in Africa, with an average population density of more than 350 people to a square kilometre (approximately half a square mile).

Over the centuries, Banyaruanda and Bakiga farmers have transformed this green and hilly land into a vast, sprawling patchwork of terraced fields, under a bewildering variety of crops; finger millet, sorghum, sweet potatoes, maize, bananas, cassava and pyrethrum. The Virunga Mountains sit like a string of islands in the middle of a boundless sea of cultivation.

It was on the southerly, Rwandan foothills of the chain that some of the bloodiest of Rwanda's civil wars of the 1950s and early 1960s took place. These wars saw the country's Bahutu majority rise up against the feudal authority of the Batutsi, the governing minority under whom the Bahutu—nearly 85 per cent of the Banyaruanda population—had served as vassals for more than 500 years.

A northern, cattle-raising people, the Batutsi, who swept into the region in the late Middle Ages from Ethiopia, were eventually deposed in 1962. More than 10,000 of them were slain in the course of the Bahutu uprising. Another 70,000 fled to the neighbouring, Ugandan foothills of the Virunga chain, where they still live today, aristocrats-turned-refugees.

In marked contrast to the Batutsi, who are the world's tallest race of people, the diminutive Batwa (the region's aboriginal inhabitants) are among the shortest, being descended directly from the Pygmies of the Ituri Forest, some 200 km (140 miles) off to the north-west. Like the Pygmies, the Batwa are essentially forest-dwelling hunter-gatherers. A mere one per cent of the Banyaruanda population, they have long since forsaken their old ways. Agricultural encroachment, coupled with the institution of national parks on the mountains, has effectively laid claim to their ancestral hunting-grounds. Today they eke out a living mainly as potters and craftsmen.

In all three countries they straddle, the high slopes of the Virunga Mountains fall within national parks. Rwanda's 15,000-ha (37,500-acre) Parc des Volcans

The crater rim of Nyiragongo.

(*Following pages*) Mikeno (left) and Karisimbi, both dormant, are the chain's loftiest volcanoes. Charred forest (foreground) is testimony to a 1981 ash-burst from Rugarambiro, in the west.

Mikeno, seen here from the Parc des Volcans in Rwanda, is the Virunga chain's most testing climbing proposition.

takes in much of the chain's southerly aspect. In the north it is contiguous with both the 20,000-ha (50,000-acre) eastern sector of Zaïre's Parc des Virungas and the small, 4,000-ha (9,000-acre) Kigezi Gorilla Sanctuary in Uganda. All three park areas, needless to say, were proclaimed in the interests of preserving the imperilled apes.

At the lower park edges, roughly 2,500 m (8,200 ft) up, the teeming farmlands give way suddenly to dank and tangled broad-leaved forests, interspersed with dripping bamboo (*Arundinaria alpina*) thickets. The riotous foliage, rife with brambles and chest-high stinging nettles, is in places virtually impenetrable. Clumps of wild celery, massed thickly around tall, swaying spikes of the rosette-leaved *Solanecio*, add to the profusion. A straggling mesh of *Galium* goosegrass sticks to, and binds, the leafy mêlée, now the tangled province of the mountain gorilla.

At about 3,000 m (9,850 ft) the dense "mixed bamboo" zone terminates abruptly. In its place comes a wide belt of enchanting "elfin" woodland, where tall, shapely *Hagenia abyssinica* trees mingle with giant, arboreal stands of the aromatic shrub St John's wort (*Hypericum revolutum*). Long, shaggy tassels of grey-green "old man's beard" (*Usnea*) lichen hang down from high boughs lined with dark cushions of dripping moss.

"Elfin" woodland is prolific only on three of the volcanoes—Mikeno, Karisimbi and Visoke. Where this thins out, at about the 3,300-m (10,825-ft) level, the Afro-alpine tussock moorlands come into their own. Here, groves of hardy tree-heather mingle on the grassy steeps with clusters of pink and white immortelles or "everlasting" (*Helichrysum*) flowers.

The summit regions of all six dormant volcanoes boast luxuriant groves of giant tree-groundsels (*Senecio spp.*), along with bold, open clusters of spike-tipped lobelias (*Lobelia bequaertii*). When they all burst into flower, the groundsels set the upper mountain slopes ablaze with their tiny yellow florets.

Of the eight Virunga Mountains, only Mikeno has ever roused any serious climbing interest. Seen from a distance, its bare central pillar looks formidable and sheer and mountaineers, during the early part of this century, were compulsively drawn towards it. The Duke of Mecklenburg, the German climber and explorer who had twice led expeditions to the Ruwenzori Mountains further to the north, was the first to tackle the forbidding pillar. The attempt, made in 1908, ended when his party was driven off the mountain by a succession of raging hailstorms.

Ensuing expeditions met with a similar fate. Even the enthusiasm of Albert, King of the Belgians, who set out to climb the pillar in the 1920s while on a visit to the Belgian Congo (as Zaïre was then), was of no avail. Magnified with each new account of failure, the severity of the ascent assumed more and more frightening proportions, until eventually Mikeno became "the Matterhorn of Africa".

In her book *Congo Eden* (1951), Mary Jobe Akeley tells of another climber, a Dr Dercheid, who in 1926 reached a point less than 70 m (230 ft) from the summit: "1,000 ft (300 m) higher," she says, "than anyone had previously reached.

"He was stopped," she writes, "by heavy storm clouds and the lateness of the hour."

It was Mrs Akeley's husband, the American naturalist Carl Akeley, who in 1925 pioneered the establishment here of the original Parc National Albert. Under Akeley the park—Africa's first—was set aside for the protection, primarily, of the Virunga mountain gorillas. Akeley himself died in 1926 while busy extending the park. His grave rests at the south-eastern foot of haggard Mikeno. His wife concludes:

> It is agreed that the two greatest difficulties encountered in the climb of Mikeno are the quantities of deep moss on the sloping rocks which will not bear the weight of a man and the extreme friability of the cliffs, where often only precarious hand and footholds can be obtained.
>
> To me from whatever location I viewed the peak, Mikeno possessed all the characteristics of a formidable mountain.[1]

To everyone's great surprise, it was a party not of dedicated mountaineers but of energetic missionaries who first stood on the barren summit of Mikeno. The party, led by Père van Hoef of the nearby Lulenga White Fathers' Mission, achieved this feat in August, 1927, at only the second attempt. The difficulties posed by the summit pillar had, needless to say, been greatly exaggerated.

The first man to climb all eight of the volcanoes was Earl Denman, the mountaineer best known for his bold, if unsuccessful, bid to scale Mount Everest in 1947. Accompanied only by two Sherpas, one of whom happened to be Tenzing Norgay of Hillary-and-Tenzing fame, Denman set out to climb mighty Everest, then still to be conquered, in the "simple way" that would later find its master exponent in Reinhold Messner, today's undisputed mountain king. But, whereas Messner conducted some of the high-altitude training for his historic 1978 "oxygenless" ascent of Everest on Africa's Kilimanjaro, Denman, ever possessed of an eccentric itch for things remote, chose the considerably lower, and thus rather more unlikely training ground of the Virunga Mountains.

Old man's beard hangs eerily from dead cedar trees.

Giant tree-groundsels enjoy a rare mass-flowering on Karisimbi, turning the whole mountainside a blazing yellow.

[1] Akeley, M. J.: *Congo Eden*, Gollancz (London), 1951.

A two-month foot safari across Africa from Bulawayo, in what was then Southern Rhodesia (now Zimbabwe), saw Denman reach the foot of the volcanoes in May 1946. His "eight-peak scheme", as he called it, took him just under a month to complete. His barefoot exploits on the volcanoes are recounted in the first part of his book *Alone to Everest*, published in 1954. First he tackled the "cooking pots", Nyiragongo and Nyamlagira:

> One night in particular was unforgettable. The tremendous bulk of Nyiragongo loomed darkly, thrown into relief by starlight, moonlight and its own red glow from above . . .
>
> The Plough, inverted, had its "handle" obscured. [It had] moved in its orbit until it was poised squarely above the glowing summit, and it all looked like a steaming Christmas pudding being poured from a huge pot. This impression was heightened by the red glow . . . which gave the effect of lighted brandy.
>
> As though this were not enough, occasional meteors hurtled across the sky like sparks from the same giant cauldron. "Cooking Pots" is indeed an appropriate term when applied to the Nyiragongo sector of the Virunga volcanoes.[2]

Next, Denman tackled Visoke and Karisimbi. The latter, the highest of the eight volcanoes, struck him as "a test of fitness more than anything else: entirely clear of forest above the Lukumi Hut and not sufficiently eroded to offer more than a hard, slogging ascent". The views from these mountains were overwhelming:

> I found myself longing, for the first and only time, for a companion to whom I could speak freely. I wanted to say "Look there, and there. Have you ever seen greater loveliness?" Or I merely wished to ask for confirmation, to make sure the fairyland of Kivu and its wonderful volcanoes really existed . . .

For Denman, as for other climbers before him, Mikeno, next in his "scheme", was technically the real *pièce de resistance*. In his mind it assumed a peculiarly intense, almost religious significance. On its "cathedral peak" he writes:

> [I] sensed that supreme elation, not of a conqueror but of a privileged human being who has been permitted to worship at this shrine mountain . . .
>
> Personally I felt that the only one to be conquered was myself. Previously I must have held a certain fear when looking at Mikeno, but having climbed it I no longer feared it. I had been intimate with it after the manner of a lover, and, as with a lover, the last barrier of reserve had been removed.[3]

This intimacy he ascribes in part to the fact that he climbed the mountain "in the simplest manner possible—barefooted every bit of the way, and groping through the mist and rain with only a pair of shorts and a ragged shirt as covering. Mikeno meant much to me—more than I can say."

Muhavura and Mgahinga, the sixth and seventh steps in Denman's quest to "be at peace with the eight Virunga mountains and with myself", presented little in the way of difficulty. Both mountains he found appealing chiefly for the magnificent views which they afford:

Silverback mountain gorilla near Djomba, on the north-western foothills of Sabinyo in Zaïre. A "silverback" is a gorilla group's dominant male, so named for his distinctive, silvery-grey dorsal hair.

---

[2] Denman, E.: *Alone to Everest*, Collins (London), 1954.
[3] Denman, E.: *op. cit.*

One incomparable panorama was of six lakes which shone like jewels; Mutanda the brightest of them and the others Mulehe, Bulera, Luhondo, Mugisha and Tshahafi. In a clearer atmosphere, Lake Bunyoni would also have been visible.

If these lakes were jewels then the countryside south-east of Kisoro [a Ugandan village just north of Muhavura] was a bed from which jewels had been plucked from their clasps, for it was pockmarked with numerous small volcanic vents, most of them identical in shape . . .[4]

Saddle moorland between Kahuzi and Biega near Bukavu in Zaïre. The Kahuzi-Biega massif is a haunt of the "eastern lowland" gorilla.

Incredibly, Denman only once encountered gorillas in all his wanderings on the Virunga Mountains. This was on Sabinyo, during the eighth, and last, of his ascents. At the time he was about 3,000 m (9,850 ft) up, in the bamboo zone, the thickest such zone on the entire mountain chain:

We heard a scrambling and a crashing ahead and to our right. Gorillas! There was no mistaking the sound of it, and the atmosphere became electric . . . For only a few seconds were there indications of intense activity, after which the sound dwindled and then ceased abruptly. We stood quite still, and the forest lapsed into complete silence.[5]

[4] Denman, E.: *op. cit.*
[5] Denman, E.: *op. cit.*

This 31-year-old silverback male presides over a large "lowland" gorilla group in Zaïre's Parc National de Kahuzi-Biega. Despite their "lowland" tag, these gorillas roam over much the same altitude range as their Virunga "mountain" cousins.

Given the denseness, and remoteness, of this its native habitat, it is little wonder that the mountain gorilla, largest of all the anthropoid apes, eluded "discovery" until as recently as 1902. For it was in that year that Oscar Beringe, a railway construction engineer on leave from Tanganyika, procured the first specimen, while hunting on the misty slopes of the volcanoes.

The subspecies, later named *Gorilla gorilla beringei* in his honour, was thus introduced to science a full half-century after its smaller and more widespread west African counterpart *Gorilla gorilla gorilla*, first made known by French explorer Paul B. du Chaillu. Far more numerous, the latter subspecies frequents lower-lying forest areas, notably in parts of Gabon, Cameroon and western Zaïre.

A third gorilla subspecies, *Gorilla gorilla graueri*, occurs in the vicinity of Mounts Kahuzi and Biega in far-eastern Zaïre, some 100 km (approximately 60 miles) south-west of the Virunga chain. Commonly known as the eastern *lowland* gorilla, this race is often confused with the mountain subspecies in that it is sometimes found at altitudes comparable with, if not actually higher than, those normally associated only with the mountain race. The lateness of the mountain gorilla's discovery has been cited by some as a compelling argument for the existence, at heights still more remote, of that altogether more elusive mountain creature, the Himalayan yeti.

The mountain gorilla's only other refuge today, besides the Virunga volcanoes, is the nearby Bwindi—or "impenetrable"—Forest in south-western Uganda, roughly 60 km (approximately 35 miles) north-east of the chain. The Virunga Mountains might still be virtually unknown outside Central Africa were it not for the burgeoning popular concern of recent years over the fate of *Gorilla gorilla beringei*, long threatened with extinction at the hands of man's encroachment on its habitat. More than anything, it is accounts of the mountain gorilla and its plight—notably those set out by George Schaller and Dian Fossey—that have brought the spectacular volcanoes to the notice of the outside world.

Here it was that Schaller, a wildlife biologist, carried out the first ever comprehensive study of mountain gorillas in their natural habitat, between 1959 and 1961. His pioneering research resulted in two books: one a scientific treatise entitled *The Mountain Gorilla: Ecology and Behaviour* and the other, of more general appeal, *The Year of the Gorilla*[6]. Schaller's study had the effect, too, of habituating groups of the wild apes to a human presence. This meant that, for the first time, visitors to the volcanoes could observe mountain gorillas at close quarters in their natural surroundings. Previously, as in Denman's experience, the apes had gone crashing off into the undergrowth on being approached.

Habituation, though, was something of a mixed blessing. More accessible to *bona fide* visitors, the apes were also more accessible to poachers. Six years after Schaller's pioneering study, the Virunga gorilla population was down by an estimated 50 per cent.

It was against this background that Dian Fossey, a 34-year-old occupational therapist from California, in the US, left her job in 1967, to commit herself full-time to studying the vanishing apes. This she did, initially, from a research base on the slopes of Mikeno, in Zaïre (then still the Democratic Republic of the Congo). Her work here was forcibly terminated after just six months, when amid growing political turmoil she was imprisoned, then brutalised, by rebellious troops from a nearby military camp. Determined to go on with her study, she proceeded, after making her escape, to establish a new base in neighbouring Rwanda, on the saddle between Karisimbi and Visoke.

The Karisoke Research Centre, as this base came to be known, was her home for the next 13 years, during which time she amassed a wealth of data on the gorillas. Her articles in *National Geographic*, the magazine which sponsored her study, fostered a worldwide concern for the mountain gorilla's survival, as did her popular book *Gorillas in the Mist*[7].

Her work at the Centre became increasingly geared towards combating the poaching menace that, despite international concern, was still exacting a heavy toll. And, whereas at first a Halloween mask had been enough to deter the poachers, her methods had to become increasingly ruthless to produce the same effect. In consequence, she made many enemies.

On December 27, 1985 Dian Fossey, aged 53, was found brutally murdered in her cabin at the Research Centre, shortly after she had returned from the US to resume her impassioned crusade on behalf of the mountain gorilla. "A deep gash ran diagonally across her forehead, over the top of her nose, and down her cheek," reads one eye-witness account. "Her eyes were wide open . . . The cabin had been ransacked. The Christmas tree alone had been spared."

Fossey was buried in the gorilla graveyard which she had created at the Centre for the victims of poaching atrocities. Her murderer was never apprehended. The gorillas, for their part, still haunt the misty, forest-clad slopes of the Virunga Mountains, like the troubled spirits of man's distant, evolutionary past.

---

[6] Both published in 1963 by The University of Chicago Press.
[7] Fossey, D.: *Gorillas in the Mist*, Hodder and Stoughton (London), 1983.

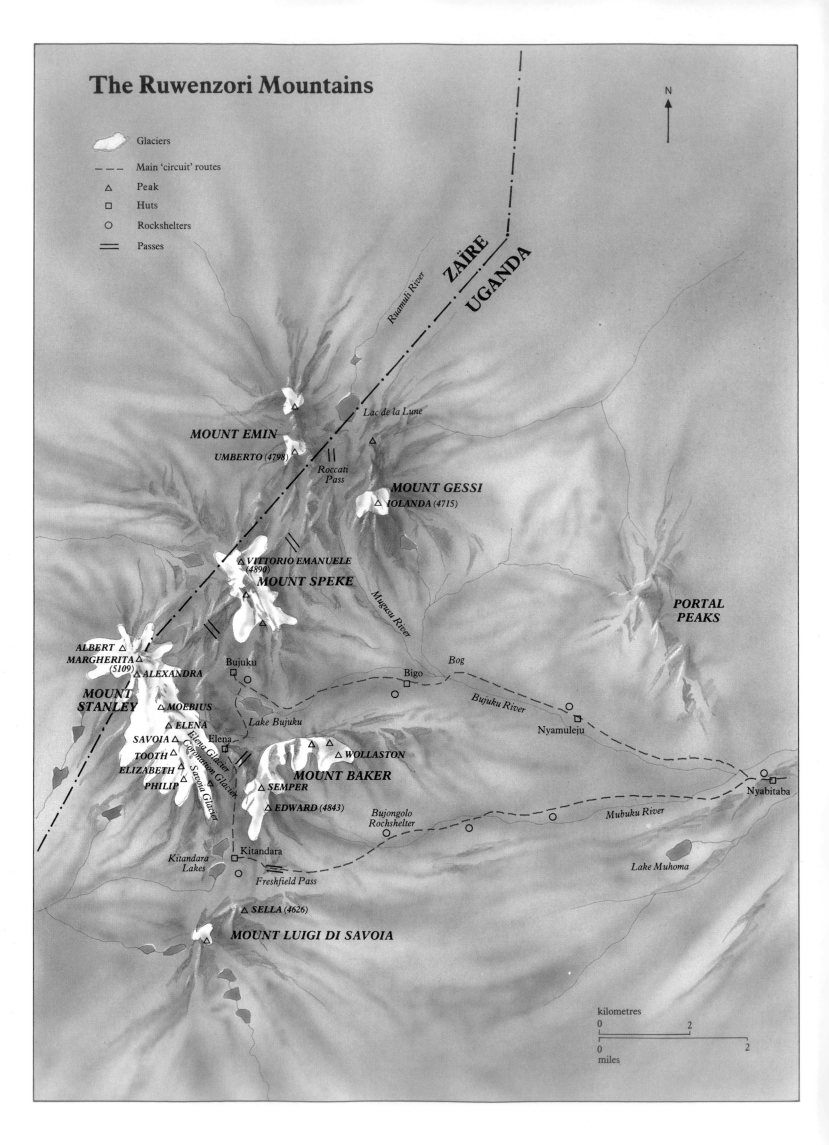

The Ruwenzori Mountains

Glaciers

Main 'circuit' routes

△ Peak

□ Huts

○ Rockshelters

Passes

N

ZAÏRE
UGANDA

Ruamuli River

Lac de la Lune

MOUNT EMIN

UMBERTO (4798) △

Roccati Pass

MOUNT GESSI

△ *IOLANDA (4715)*

△ *VITTORIO EMANUELE (4890)*

MOUNT SPEKE

Mugusu River

PORTAL PEAKS

ALBERT △
MARGHERITA (5109) △
△ *ALEXANDRA*

MOUNT STANLEY

△ *MOEBIUS*

Bujuku □ ○

Lake Bujuku

Bigo □

Bog

Bujuku River

○

○ □
Nyamuleju

△ *ELENA*

SAVOIA △   Elena □
TOOTH △

Elena Glacier
Coronation Glacier

△ *WOLLASTON*

MOUNT BAKER

○ □
Nyabitaba

ELIZABETH △
PHILIP △

Savoia Glacier

△ *SEMPER*

△ *EDWARD (4843)*

Bujongolo Rochshelter ○

○   ○
Mubuku River

Kitandara Lakes

Kitandara □
○

Freshfield Pass

Lake Muhoma

△ *SELLA (4626)*

MOUNT LUIGI DI SAVOIA

kilometres
0   2

0   2
miles

2 · Icy Mountains of the Moon: The Ruwenzori Mountains

Gordon Boy

The permanent white mantle of snow and ice that covers and surrounds the megalithic high peaks of the Ruwenzori Range gleams coldly underneath a glaring equatorial sun. Huge fleecy cornices of icy rime mushroom out into space from sheer, ice-encrusted rock faces, creating massive crystal awnings that appear to defy the laws of gravity. And rolled out down the mountainsides from ice-caves at the bases of the peaks lie the glistening wet tongues of the Ruwenzori glaciers.

It does seem hard to believe that the equator should be no more than 50 km (approximately 30 miles) away. But then, the Ruwenzori has a long history of confounding expectations; a penchant for stretching the limits of the credible. The phenomenal gigantism inherent in the range's Afro-alpine flora is perhaps the most striking manifestation of this tendency. For it is here that the plants of the east and central African mountains reach the acme of their development. The tree-heathers (*Philippia* and *Erica spp.*), lobelias, senecios and immortelles of the Ruwenzori are colossal by comparison with those of other mountains.

The stimulus for this extraordinary growth rests in the combination of the equatorial heat with a rainfall that in some months exceeds 400 mm (approximately 16 inches), making the Ruwenzori one of the wettest mountain areas in the world.

In the range's many deep, moraine-blocked valleys the exceptionally heavy year-round precipitation is soaked up relentlessly by an immense natural sponge system consisting of a plethora of spectacular lime-green, yellow and russet-coloured sphagnum and other mosses. Here, even the lowly bryophytes achieve a variety and a profuseness that is unsurpassed anywhere else in Africa.

Massed around huge tussock islands of *Carex runsorrensis* sedge, this perennially saturated sponge forms some of the continent's most extensive and intractable bogland. Run-off from this moss/bog zone, as it is called, is responsible for transforming the clear, icy streams fed by the melt-off from the glaciers above into cascading rivers which in turn serve as the major sources of the waters of the Nile. Giant, thumb-thick earthworms (*Lumbricus spp.*), some of them more than three-quarters of a metre (approximately 2 ft) long, burrow and squirm mindlessly through the damp, muddy earth on the banks of these turbulent, Nile-bound rivers.

This strange realm—the realm of the Ruwenzori or "Hill of Rain"—is 110 km (approximately 70 miles) long and nearly 50 km (approximately 30 miles) broad, and straddles the border between Uganda and Zaïre, at the heart of equatorial Africa. It rises to a central mass of six great mountains, whose names—Stanley, Speke, Baker, Emin, Gessi and Luigi di Savoia—read like a pantheon of early central African exploration. Together, these six mountains boast a total of 24 major peaks higher than 4,600 m (15,092 ft).

Tangle of groundsel, lobelia and moss.

Giant earthworm.

The highest peak is Margherita, on Mount Stanley, which in reaching up to 5,109 m (16,763 ft) renders the Ruwenzori the third highest massif in Africa, surpassed only by Kilimanjaro and Mount Kenya. Two of the other Ruwenzori peaks—namely Alexandra at 5,091 m (16,703 ft) and Albert at 5,087 m (16,690 ft), standing one on either side of Margherita on Mount Stanley—also rise above the magical 5,000-m (16,400-ft) mark.

For all their great height, the snow-capped Ruwenzori peaks are seldom visible from the surrounding plains. The thick blanket of cloud that habitually hangs over the range, coupled with the haze created by smoke from the myriad fires kindled on the plains themselves, is such that people can live and work in the vicinity for many months without ever catching so much as a single glimpse of the lofty, snow-topped summits.

Concealed thus, it is little wonder that the Ruwenzori was the last of Africa's great massifs to reveal itself to the early white explorers. And even when in May 1888 the cloud blanket did roll back for long enough for the explorer Henry Morton Stanley to be able to furnish the outside world with confirmation of the range's existence, the view, as Stanley set it down in his book *In Darkest Africa* (1890), had all the qualities of a phantom vision:

> While looking to the south-east and meditating on the events of the last month, my eyes were directed by a boy to a mountain said to be covered with salt and I saw a peculiar shaped cloud of a most beautiful silver colour . . .
>
> I became conscious that what I gazed upon was not the image or semblance of a vast mountain but the solid substance of a real one, with its summit covered in snow.

Henry Morton Stanley.

The sighting (Stanley's second, though at the time he clearly failed to recognise it as such) came while the explorer was encamped near the shores of Lake Albert. This was during the course of the expedition he had led from the west coast of Africa with the goal of "rescuing" Emin Pasha, the governor of Equatoria, who was then presumed to have been cut off in the heart of the continent by the Mahdist uprisings in the Sudan.

The Ruwenzori snows had in fact been spotted a month earlier by two of the officers accompanying Stanley, namely A. J. Mounteney Jephson and T. H. Parke. But it was Stanley's account that was finally to break the spell of uncertainty and mystery which had for so long been cast around the very existence, let alone the form and whereabouts, of the range's great snow peaks.

Moreover, it was from Stanley's "Runzori", apparently an amalgam of such local names as the Lunyoro "Rwenjura" and the Lukonjo "Rwenzururu" and "Runssoro" (all meaning, loosely, "Hill of Rain") as he had managed to glean in the course of his travels in the area, that the range's present name came about.

Stanley had himself first seen the massif 12 years earlier, while on the second of his central African expeditions. The "faint view of an enormous blue mass afar off" which he describes in *Through the Dark Continent* (1878) as having caught his eye in January 1876 was almost certainly the first sighting by a white man of the Ruwenzori Mountains.

At the time, Stanley had promptly named the mass "Mount Gordon Bennett", after the proprietor of the *New York Herald*, which in conjunction with *The Daily Telegraph* (London) had undertaken to finance the expedition. Little did he realise that the snow mountain he found himself looking at in 1888 was this very same Mount Gordon Bennett.

Between these two sightings of Stanley's the massif had of course been glimpsed by other travellers. Among them was the Italian explorer Romolo Gessi who, while making the first ever recorded circumnavigation of Lake Albert in April 1876, had noticed "a strange vision in the sky" to the south of

(*Opposite*) Mount Speke, from an ice-cave on the Stanley Plateau.

(*Following pages*) The northern peaks of Mount Stanley, Margherita (right) and Alexandra, are the highest on the Ruwenzori range. They were first scaled in 1906 by a formidable climbing team led by Italy's Prince Luigi Amedeo di Savoia, Duke of the Abruzzi.

the lake. To this vision he had given the name "Mount Modrog" (presumably a veiled, inverted tribute to General Gordon, the Sudan-based Equatorial governor in whose service Gessi was then employed).

By the time the Ruwenzori had started playing havoc with the observations of the nineteenth-century explorers, the existence somewhere in the heart of Africa of just such a mountain range had already been postulated for more than 2,000 years by some of the world's foremost thinkers and geographers as a solution to what was to become the greatest and most enduring natural mystery of all time: the location of the sources of the Nile.

As early as 500 BC, the Greek dramatist and poet Aeschylus had written of "Egypt nurtured by the snows". And in 450 BC Herodotus, the father of Greek history, had suggested that the Nile rose from a spring fed by the waters of a bottomless lake set between two sharp-pointed peaks called Crophi and Mophi. Not long afterwards in 350 BC, the philosopher Aristotle had declared the source of the Nile to be "the Silver Mountain".

Then, in c. AD 120, the Syrian geographer Marinus of Tyre had recounted the remarkable story of a Greek merchant named Diogenes who claimed to have arrived, following a 25-day journey inland from the east coast of Africa in the middle of the first century AD, at "two great lakes and the snowy range of mountains whence the Nile draws its twin sources".

It was from this account of Diogenes' legendary adventure that in c. AD 150 Claudius Ptolemy, the most distinguished geographer and astronomer of his age, had gone on to produce his celebrated early map of Africa. On it the two great lakes, placed side by side just to the south of the equator, are shown to be watered by the high *Lunae Montes* or "Mountains of the Moon".

No name could better have captured the spirit of mystery and fascination that was to grow up around the proposed mountainous source of the great river. And when, nearly 1,700 years later, the first European explorers ventured into Africa's uncharted interior, intent upon solving once and for all the lingering enigma of the Nile's origin, it was for Ptolemy's "Mountains of the Moon" they searched.

One by one, all the major East and Central African massifs they encountered in their wanderings, among them the Kilimanjaro, Mount Kenya and the Virunga, or Mufumbiro, Volcanoes, were at first enthusiastically proclaimed to be the mountains to which Ptolemy had drawn attention.

But it was the Ruwenzori Mountains that were to lay the most insistent claim to being the fabled *Lunae Montes*. For, while none of the drainage from either Kilimanjaro or Mount Kenya (and only a small part of that coming off the Virunga Mountains) flows into the Nile, the streams that pour down off the Ruwenzori provide the mighty river, mainly via the Semliki valley and Lake Albert, with its largest and most dependable water catchment.

The Ruwenzori are, at any rate, now universally identified with the "Mountains of the Moon". The age-old romantic heritage they have acquired in consequence must surely rank among the richest and most intriguing relating to any of the world's great mountains.

Just how the range came into being in the first place, however, is still something of a mystery. Rising from the Western Rift System's eastern scarp, the Ruwenzori take the form of an enormous horst or fault-block: a mass of rock tilted and thrust up in a series of huge ridges between near-parallel faults in the earth's crust. Though integrally bound up with the development of the Western Rift System, itself the result of a large-scale subsidence between the cracks caused by the parallel faulting, the exact mechanism of the Ruwenzori upthrust remains obscure, as does the nature of its connection with the Rift's formation.

Both events are clearly the result of considerable imbalances in the forces at work here in the earth's crust. And the frequent earth tremors that occur in the vicinity confirm that the rifting and uplifting processes are still in progress today.

The upthrust of the Ruwenzori is thought to have begun little more than 2 million years ago: an estimate that places the range among the youngest of all the east and central African massifs, with an age *as a mountain form* that is perhaps only one-third that of Mount Kenya.

Paradoxically, however, the Ruwenzori is materially very much older than any of the region's big volcanic massifs, being composed almost entirely of Pre-Cambrian basement rocks. Some of its granitic gneisses, quartzites, schists and other metamorphic rocks have been shown, meanwhile, to be up to 1,800 million years old, *i.e.* more than a hundred times older than any of the rocks found on Mount Kenya.

The fact that the Ruwenzori are not of extrusive volcanic origin is in itself something of an anomaly in that their surroundings, in particular the low-lying flats of the Ruwenzori (formerly Queen Elizabeth) National Park around Lake Edward and Lake George, to the south of the range, have been the scene of some of Africa's most violent volcanic activity of recent times, and are in consequence extensively pock-marked with explosion craters.

If the range's identity bred confusion in the minds of the early white explorers, its topography was to prove utterly bewildering to those who first endeavoured, in the 1890s and very early 1900s, to come to terms with the mysteries of the great snow-covered peaks.

Even the Bakonjo and Banande peoples who, by this time, of course, had been living and hunting on the slopes of the Ruwenzori for centuries, possessed only scant knowledge of the range's snowy upper reaches. These heights were believed by the Bakonjo, the aboriginal inhabitants of the slopes on the eastern, or Ugandan, side of the range, to be the hallowed province of the powerful deity Kitasamba, who along with his four wives, the most favoured among whom was called Nyabubuya, had reputedly held court among the Ruwenzori peaks since the very beginnings of time.

But for the supreme Creator of the Universe, Kitasamba had always been the most important, and most feared, of all the Bakonjo deities. And the nemesis that lay in store for anyone presumptuous enough to trespass on the god's lofty domain was something the Bakonjo people knew only too well. The trespasser, they said, would be smitten with terrible headaches; fits of shivering and nausea, and swellings on, and loss of feeling in, his fingers and toes: all clearly symptoms of high-altitude exposure and mountain sickness.

Fear of thus incurring the wrath of Kitasamba had, understandably, made the Bakonjo extremely loath to venture up into the Ruwenzori snows. The lower slopes of the Ruwenzori, by contrast, had long been familiar territory to the Bakonjo who, in the course of their hunting and trapping forays, had given expressive local names to all the rivers, valleys, lakes, caves, rockshelters and other topographical features they habitually encountered or made use of there.

For the Europeans who first set their sights on climbing the Ruwenzori peaks, the range's mysterious allure was heightened by the tales related of the mountains by the Batoro, Banyoro and other tribes of the region to the east and north-east of the range. The Italian explorer and roving Equatorial envoy Gaetano Casati, before whom the snowy crest of "the great mountain of the Vacongio" had appeared in April 1889, reported in his book *Ten Years in Equatoria and the Return with Emin Pasha* (1891) that "the people of Unyoro say that no one who has attempted its mysteries has ever returned . . . Cold and horrible monsters are said to rule over it," he wrote.

But Casati, while professing "a keener desire than ever to solve the mystery", never actually attempted to do so. Within months however of his sighting of the Ruwenzori's "gigantic Alpine form", the first of many attempts by European

The south ridge of Mount Baker looks down over the Kitandara Lakes. The distant peaks of Mount Luigi di Savoia notch the skyline.

climbers at unveiling the range's well-kept secrets was launched. This saw Lieutenant W. G. Stairs, one of the officers on Stanley's third central African expedition, reach a height of some 3,230 m (10,600 ft) on the northern flank of the 4,798-m (15,740-ft) Mount Emin, itself the northernmost of the six great Ruwenzori Mountains.

Although several expeditions followed in the 1890s, it was not until 1900 that the presence of the Ruwenzori glaciers became widely known. This followed reports by the British zoologist J. E. S. Moore who, early in that year, had reached the two large glaciers at the head of the Mubuku Valley on the eastern flank of Mount Baker, which was then still widely believed to carry the highest of the Ruwenzori peaks.

By the end of 1905, the picture which had emerged of the Ruwenzori peak region was still as muddled as ever. Climbers' accounts of the region's topography were full of discrepancies. And there was no consensus as to how many mountains or groups of summits there were above the snow-line, or even as to which, and how high, the highest peaks really were.

The confusion was due largely to the vastness of the range itself, presenting as it does a far more extensive Alpine area than do any of the other major African mountains. But other factors such as persistently inclement weather and extremely poor visibility, coupled with the difficulty of finding porters who would be prepared to brave the unknown heights, doubtless also played a part. Vain efforts to identify specific peaks by local names that later turned out to be no more than vague generalisations evidently further complicated matters.

The picture available a year later, *i.e.* by the end of 1906, could not have been more different however. For in the course of this one year, the greatest by far in

Freshfield Pass on the southern flank of Mount Baker.

the annals of Ruwenzori exploration, much of the topographical confusion was systematically cleared up. It was in February 1906 that the first recorded ascent of any of the range's major snow peaks was achieved. This saw A. F. R. Wollaston and R. B. Woosnam, both members of the British Museum's first Ruwenzori expedition, scale the topmost point on the eastern end of the long, curved summit ridge of Mount Baker.

The peak in question, since known as Wollaston peak, is 4,627 m (15,180 ft) high. Its prominence from the upper Mubuku Valley, the then favoured eastern approach to the snows, is such that until the Museum expedition it was widely thought to be the highest of the Ruwenzori peaks. Once on the peak, the two climbers realised, without even getting a clear view, that this was far from being the topmost pinnacle of the range. In fact, there are at least 20 peaks on the Ruwenzori, two of them on the western extremity of the same Mount Baker summit ridge, that are higher.

Not surprisingly perhaps, it took a team of dedicated mountaineers and an expedition equipped in the grand Himalayan style finally to unveil the secrets of these hidden peaks. Such was the expedition mounted in June 1906 by the royal Italian mountaineer and explorer Prince Luigi Amedeo di Savoia, better known simply as the Duke of the Abruzzi.

His formidable team included the well-known Alpine guides Joseph Petigax, César Ollier, Joseph Brocherel and Laurent Petigax (the latter two serving, in this instance, as high-altitude porters) and the renowned mountain photographer Vittorio Sella. Also in the party were the surveyor Umberto Cagni and the geologist Dr Alessandro Roccati, as well as four other Europeans and an army of about 150 African porters.

Dwarfed by huge candyfloss-like rime cornice, Armand Hughes-d'Aeth negotiates a way up Margherita, on Mount Stanley.

The sun shone on this expedition, quite literally, from the very outset. The half an hour or so of exceptionally clear weather that the advance party was able to enjoy while on the Mount Baker summit ridge gave the expedition an auspicious start of a kind previously only dreamed of. The party was thus able to use this vantage point, which under such rare conditions of perfect visibility affords fine views of all the range's major peaks, to coordinate a strategy that was to result in the accomplishment of 30 ascents within a period of just 40 days: a quite remarkable achievement.

First, the Duke and his guides traversed the ridge itself and climbed Mount Baker's two highest points, namely the 4,843-m (15,889-ft) Edward peak (whose name, after King Edward VII of Great Britain, was carried over from previous expeditions) and the 4,795-m (15,730-ft) peak alongside it, which they called Semper peak, after the European architect Prof. Gottfried Semper.

The party then turned its attention to Mount Stanley. From the expedition's fixed base camp at Bujongolo—a large natural rockshelter near the head of the Mubuku Valley—the climbers rounded Mount Baker's deceptively mild southern slope, via what they called the Freshfield Pass (after Douglas Freshfield, the Alpine Club president who had unsuccessfully attempted to unveil the Ruwenzori's mysteries the year before).

Once across this pass, which in reality is no more than a lengthy stretch of typical Ruwenzori bogland, they made their way down into the steep Kitandara Valley, where they camped beside the still, leaden waters of the lower and bigger of the two wonderfully scenic Kitandara lakes.

On reaching the bank of terminal moraine at the head of this valley, the climbers negotiated an oblique route up the side of the rocky spur linking Mount Stanley with Mount Baker and established, near the edge of the Elena Glacier, the base that was to become known as "Ridge Camp".

Through granting ready access to the great central expanse of the Stanley Ice Plateau, this camp was ideally positioned. And, within a day of reaching Mount Stanley, that formidable team of Abruzzi, Petigax (J.), Ollier and Brocherel completed first ascents of both the Ruwenzori's two highest peaks, which they named Margherita and Alexandra (after the respective queens of Umberto I of Italy and Edward VII of Great Britain). The date of this triumph was June 18, 1906.

The ascent of Margherita, undertaken in failing visibility, was an especially impressive feat inasmuch as the route taken by the party, a traverse from Alexandra, via the crevasse-cleft snow col between the two peaks, must then have bordered on impossibility. The rime cornices on Margherita would then, as a rule, have been much larger and more numerous than they are today. Abruzzi's team, we know, had to hack a near-vertical passage through the cornices in order to reach the summit: a feat not repeated for almost half a century afterwards. More recently, however, this direct route, technically classed as "Grade III to impossible, according to cornices", has been climbed several times.

Abruzzi and his guides rounded off their conquest of Mount Stanley with ascents of two of the major peaks to the south of the Ice Plateau. These peaks they called Savoia and Elena (the latter, like the glacier below it, being named in honour of the queen of Vittorio Emanuele III). At 4,977 m (16,330 ft) and 4,968 m (16,300 ft), these are, respectively, the fourth and fifth highest peaks on the Ruwenzori.

After leaving Ridge Camp, the party went on to make the first recorded ascent of nearby Mount Speke, whose 4,890-m (16,042-ft) summit peak Abruzzi called Vittorio Emanuele. This peak has since become the most frequently climbed of all the range's major peaks.

The topmost peak on Mount Emin, to the north, was the party's next major

(*Opposite*) Clive Ward leads the crux pitch during the first ascent of the north-eastern Ridge of Savoia, the highest of Mount Stanley's southern peaks.

success. And, after having scaled this 4,798-m (15,740-ft) pinnacle, which the Duke called Umberto, after the Italian crown prince, the tireless, high-altitude explorers began the long journey back to their base camp.

Their colleagues with the main body of the expedition, meanwhile, had been far from idle. Sella, for instance, had led a small party up onto the Stanley Plateau and made the first ascent of Moebius, the isolated, 4,918-m (16,134-ft) pinnacle of rock protruding from the middle of this gently sloping open plain of snow and ice. Sella later also scaled Mount Luigi di Savoia, the spectacular northern aspect of which dominates the horizon to the south of the boggy Freshfield Pass. The mountain's 4,626-m (15,178-ft) summit peak now bears his name.

Sella's magnificent photographs, in particular his series of snowscapes taken from the Stanley Plateau, reveal a far heavier and more extensive covering of snow and ice than is found today on the Ruwenzori. In fact, several of the glaciers seen by the Abruzzi party have since disappeared altogether. Others, like the Elena Glacier and the main Speke glaciers, have been receding in the meantime at an average rate of more than six metres a year. Continuing glacial retreat, a process that has been under way for at least the past 15,000 years, presumably as a result of the intensifying global "greenhouse effect", will in time doubtless deprive the Ruwenzori of still more of its glaciers.

Having briefly rejoined the rest of his expedition, Abruzzi struck off again to the north with two of his Alpine guides. The result was the first recorded ascent of Mount Gessi, the one great Ruwenzori mountain that had hitherto eluded his team of mountaineers. The ascent of Mount Gessi's 4,715-m (15,470-ft) summit peak, named Iolanda after the Italian princess and daughter of Vittorio Emanuele III, served as a fitting climax to what had clearly been a remarkably successful expedition. The high, central peak region of the Ruwenzori was, after all, no longer *terra incognita*.

More than 80 years later, in January, 1987, Clive and I set out from the village of Ibanda, as hundreds of others had done before us, on a journey that would take us up into the icy heart of this central peak region.

Set in the Mubuku Valley at the eastern foot of the mountains, Ibanda lies within easy reach of the steep, wet paths that afford the simplest and most direct access to the peaks. The village itself is barely 1,500 m (4,921 ft) above sea level; a reminder that the climb in prospect is considerable, even from here. Earlier, we had spent the best part of three days tripping back and forth between Ibanda and the nearby town of Kasese, making arrangements for the engagement of porters and buying food and supplies enough for a month-long sojourn on the Mountains of the Moon.

Kasese is itself little more than a dusty village. Yet, because it is served by public air, road and rail transport, it has become a popular, if necessary, stopover for pilgrims to the Ruwenzori. And during the two main climbing seasons, which span the December–February and June–August periods when there is generally least rain and snow on the mountains, the town is host to visitors from all over the world.

As with most visitors, our first step after reaching Kasese had been to make contact at Ibanda with John Matte, the area's long-serving one-man porters' employment agency. Matte, now in his late sixties, had given us a rousing welcome, remembering Clive from his three previous visits to the Ruwenzori. We had then discussed with Matte our expedition strategy over a mug of sweet, African-style tea. Our plan this time was to stick to the popular "circuit". This would take us up to the Elena Glacier via the Bujuku Valley and then back down again along the route pioneered by Abruzzi and his party.

In allocating a full month to the round trip—a trip for which a week is generally considered adequate—we hoped to spend three or four nights in each

Bakonjo porter.

Porters cross the Bujuku River on the way up to the Nyamuleju Hut, on the main eastern approach to the Ruwenzori snows.

of the huts along the way, while having plenty of time in which to bivouac between huts, as and when we saw fit. Located at six strategic points on the circuit, the huts are the legacy of the Mountain Club of Uganda, which disbanded in the 1970s after nearly 30 years of active service, a casualty of Uganda's troubled years under Idi Amin. Built in the late 1940s and early 1950s, the huts are now dilapidated structures that in some cases are barely even habitable.

After discussing the logistics of our expedition, Matte had, as he put it, "selected" a headman for the journey. This headman, Zaruloni Bwambale, had in turn set about the task of "selecting" the porters, three to accompany us over the whole circuit, and a further five to link up with us only over those stretches where extra carrying capacity would be required. Matte's son, Dezi, would also be joining us throughout, as interpreter. Our expedition would thus be seven-strong at times, at others up to 12-strong.

The equipping even of a modest expedition like this can be a complicated, time-consuming business. But in retrospect, even this forms an integral part of the Ruwenzori's appeal. For, unlike other east and central African mountains, the range has remained fundamentally untameable, a wilderness so vast that the need for an old-style expedition and the romance which this entails still live on.

The haggling that had broken out among our porters over the initial allocation of loads had effectively put paid to our hopes of an early start. But I had been told that a mock near-mutiny is the standard prelude to a departure for the Ruwenzori peaks. In any event, it was approaching mid-morning by the time we finally set off from Ibanda on the first leg of our journey, which would take us up as far as the Nyabitaba Hut.

Climbing steadily up the lower Mubuku Valley, we passed initially through grassland and through fields of beans, cassava, millet, bananas and other crops planted by Bakonjo peasant farmers. The climb then steepened and after about three and a half hours of walking we finally entered the cool sanctuary

Pathside shrine, erected by trappers to appease hunting gods Nyawirika and Kahiyi. Symbolic offerings of eggs, bananas and sugar cane are deposited by passing hunters.

of the montane forest. Now only a steep, bracken-covered ridge bearing some magnificent *Podocarpus* trees (*Podocarpus milanjianus*) stood between us and the hut.

At the foot of this ridge, on either side of the path, we noticed two small, conical enclosures made from sticks and thatched with bracken, both just half a metre or so off the ground. On nests of grass inside each of these strange constructs we found an egg, flanked by the two halves of a peeled banana, and in one there was an old stick of sugar cane as well, blackened with age.

"These are shrines which are put here," Dezi explained, "to keep the Bakonjo hunting gods happy, so that hunting on the mountains will be good. They are called *syondekere*, and after a successful hunt a piece of dried meat from the hunted animal may be left here."

The hunting gods themselves, he said, were "two very old men, a father called Nyawirika and his son Kahiyi". Pipes made out of banana stems and leaves were sometimes also stored in these shrines, he told us, to be smoked by passing hunters. The Lukonjo name "Nyabitaba", meaning "mother of tobacco", could refer to the smoking by hunters of similar pipes such as might have been kept in the rockshelter near the hut which now bears this name.

Once actually at Nyabitaba, we set about devising a strategy for tackling the first objective of our trip: that of photographing the brilliant, iridescent crimson-, green- and blue-coloured Ruwenzori turaco (*Ruwenzorornis johnstoni johnstoni*). For Clive, this had long been something of a challenge.

"As one of the true symbols of the Ruwenzori forest, I had always hoped," he had told me, "to see the bird pictured somewhere in the Ruwenzori literature. Not finding it there, I decided to try to get the shots myself."

In fact, this particular bird, set apart from its closest relatives by the crimson splashes on its nape and chest, lives only on the Ruwenzori, though an allied race of the same bird does occur in the forests skirting the Virunga volcanoes, further south.

After four days however our camera hunt had begun to look utterly hopeless. On the advice of one of our porters, Jumado, we had spent two of these days in the Lake Muhoma area, some distance higher up the Nyabitaba ridge. But here, as around the hut itself, periodic flashes of blood-red wings afloat among the tree-tops high above our heads were our only glimpses of the bird.

While picking our way through the dense bamboo around Lake Muhoma we had managed, however, to startle a group of rare black-and-white Ruwenzori colobus monkeys (*Colobus angolensis ruwenzorii*), handsome creatures which must rank among the real aristocrats of the simian world. Yet as photographic subjects these shy animals had proved every bit as elusive as the turacos.

Lake Muhoma itself, at nearly 3,000 m (9,843 ft) above sea level, is the lowest of the range's many beautiful lakes. Flanked by ridges of lateral moraine (the Nyabitaba ridge making up one flank), this tranquil, bamboo-fringed expanse of water is thought to have been formed 15,000 years ago, in the wake of the glacial retreat that has been in progress here since Pleistocene times.

On getting back to Nyabitaba following our brief lakeside interlude we found the area around the hut teeming with people. Two large parties of Bakonjo trappers, one on its way up to the moorlands, the other on its way down, were "taking tea" here, Dezi told us, and exchanging news. Our porters themselves were soon part of the proceedings, lost in the smoke of the struggling communal fire. When Zaruloni reappeared after about half an hour, it was to tell us that the returning trappers had "seen plenty of *sukurru* (the onomatopoeic Lukonjo name for the turaco, whose call follows a distinctive *sukurru-kurrr-kurrr* sequence) up at Nyamuleju".

Our climb the next day to the Nyamuleju hut took almost four hours, down through dense bamboo to the confluence of the Mubuku and Bujuku rivers to

Forest of giant heather and *Rapanea* shrubbery in the moss/bog zone.

The delicate ground orchid *Disa stairsii* was named after Lieutenant W. G. Stairs, who collected a type-specimen on the Ruwenzori in 1889, while journeying across Africa with the explorer Henry Morton Stanley.

begin with, then across these rivers and up along the northern bank of the Bujuku River. On passing through a scenic woodland area dominated by huge hagenia trees, some of the range's spectacular Afro-alpine plants began to make their first appearance, in the form of the tree-heathers, St John's worts, lobelias and immortelles. But perhaps the most striking plant we saw here was the delicate, coral-pink ground orchid, *Disa stairsii*.

It is from the pale grey-green streamers of lichen which hang from all the trees here that the Nyamuleju hut gets its name: Lukonjo for "Place of Beards". The fact that most of the *Rapanea rhododendronoides* trees we passed in approaching the hut were laden with ripe purple berries was to prove a good omen for our turaco quest. For over the next few days these trees were simply alive with the birds.

But the weather turned against us, with a combination of unseasonally heavy rainfall and almost constant mist. Confined to the hut for virtually two whole days, I read the Osmaston and Pasteur *Guide to the Ruwenzori* (1972), the only book we had with us, from cover to cover at least twice. And if ever there is rucksack space enough for only one book on a hike among the Mountains of the Moon this little blue book must get the vote. It is a mine of fascinating information.

Clive, meanwhile, built a photographic hide a few hundred metres downhill from the hut. The resulting heather-and-lichen creation looked out on a carefully chosen perch, decked with a "bait" of the choicest *Rapanea* fruit that could be found. But, after two more days of mainly gloomy weather and many long and unrewarding hours of seclusion in this blind, even he lost all patience with the "hunt". We packed in readiness for a departure the next morning for the Bujuku huts, a five-hour climb up the valley from Nyamuleju.

Jumado had by this time already gone back down to Ibanda to see to the loading and bringing up of our remaining supplies, left in John Matte's care. We had arranged to meet up with him again in two days' time at Cooking Pot Cave, a prominent, boarded-up rockshelter just below the site of the Bujuku huts.

What happened next was quite astonishing. On chancing to look up from

The Ruwenzori turaco.

where we lay sprawled out beside the hut awaiting the onset of evening we saw, on a small *Rapanea* bush barely seven metres (approximately 22 ft) away, a magnificent specimen of the turaco: easily the best view we had yet had of the bird. Our reaction, though, was an absolute fiasco. The unpacking of the camera gear seemed to take an eternity, as did the search for the necessary fast film. Then Clive contrived to trip over his own tripod, and the camera's motor drive facility jammed . . .

And yet through all this the bird miraculously continued feeding, and Clive was able after all to get some photographs. "Not the best," he said, "but some reward at least for all the trouble."

The walk to the Bujuku huts took us up through a forest of giant heathers to the lower of the Bujuku Valley's two arduous peat bogs. The heathers, here reaching heights of up to 14 m (45 ft), are among the most exaggerated of all the Ruwenzori's gigantic plant forms. Their twisted limbs, heavy with luxuriant bands of thick, dripping mosses, are the stuff of fairytales, statuesque and colourful when bathed in sunlight, eerie and foreboding when encountered in a mist.

The crossing of the lower Bigo Bog was an adventure in itself. The unseasonally heavy downpours had left this wetter than we had expected, and our attempts at getting across on the treacherous "stepping stones" provided by the scattered tussocks of sedge, a tactic calling for many big, hopeful leaps, soon had to be abandoned. Instead, we ended up having to wade, up to our thighs in some places, through the moss-covered expanse of cold, dark mud.

Protruding from the bog are the distinctive stout green flower "spikes" of some particularly fine, giant specimens of lobelia, often with thick clumps of the white-flowered immortelle massed around their purple-tinged leaf rosettes. This striking combination more than made up for the manifold discomforts of "bog-hopping".

Stopping briefly for tea near Bigo hut, 3,445 m (11,300 ft) up, we again came upon some of the Bakonjo trappers we had seen the week before at Nyabitaba. Since then, we learned through Dezi, they had been "keeping mostly to the Mugusu Valley, but the hunting there was not good". Still, we noticed that they did have some hyrax meat to show for their efforts.

The Ruwenzori hyrax (*Dendrohyrax arboreus ruwenzorii*), is now virtually the sole quarry of the trappers, there being little else left to hunt on the mountains. Peculiar to the range, this small, furry creature, often likened to an outsized guinea-pig, is peculiar among tree hyraxes in having taken to living on the ground, specifically among tumbled rocks well above the tree-line, at altitudes of up to 4,450 m (14,600 ft). Its "lowland" relatives, by contrast, live mainly in the canopies of rain forests.

The animal's distinctive call, a gradual *crrrk-crrrk-crrrk* like the winding up of a primitive alarm-clock, followed by the prolonged, deafening screech of this alarm's going off, still sometimes splits the silence of the Ruwenzori night. It is an unforgettable sound when heard during one of those long periods of insomnia that are so much a feature of nights spent at the higher altitudes.

Had we had time, we might have struck north from the Bigo hut, up to the head of the Mugusu Valley and over the pass leading down to the Lac de la Lune, set between the steep, jagged ridges of mounts Emin and Gessi.

The sharp, pointed outlines of these summits, when seen from the north, inspired Noel Humphreys, the British doctor who in the late 1920s and early 1930s first thoroughly explored those parts of the range lying to the north and south of the central peak region, to associate the lake with Herodotus' "bottom-less" source of the Nile. In fact, the Ruanoli River which springs from this secluded lake *is* one of the Nile's many sources. And this, coupled with the remarkable degree to which Emin and Gessi seem to tie in with Herodotus' depiction of Crophi and Mophi, is uncanny, to say the least.

We were still pondering over this mystery when we were obliged to start

The Ruwenzori hyrax, prized for its meat and skin, is the main quarry of Bakonjo trappers.

The north face of Mount Baker from the upper Bujuku Valley, where the giant groundsel is at its most profuse.

wading again, this time across the muddy wastes of the upper Bigo Bog. Having followed us up the steep path from the hut, the trappers chatted noisily with our porters as we made the crossing. Their boisterous, fawn-coloured mongrel, Simba, for once humbled by conditions underfoot, was soon covered in the black mud.

Two hours later we finally got up to the Bujuku huts, after skirting the muddy, northern shore of Lake Bujuku, at the valley head. It is around this lake that the range's bizarre Afro-alpine plants really come into their own. The groundsel (*Senecio adnivalis*) here assumes colossal proportions, forming thick "lollipop" forests, while the tall, slender spikes of *Lobelia wollastonii*, unquestionably one of high-altitude equatorial gigantism's weirdest embodiments, stand idly by, like silvery-blue triffids waiting for their time to walk about.

Another striking plant found at this altitude is the endemic *Hypericum bequaertii*, a tree up to 10 m (approximately 30 ft) in height whose deep orange, goblet-shaped flowers contrast markedly with the splayed, yellow blossoms of the more familiar St John's wort trees we had encountered earlier at Nyamuleju.

The Bujuku huts, 3,962 m (13,000 ft) up, are virtually surrounded by the Hill of Rain's three highest mountains: Stanley, Speke and Baker. Yet in our few days here we caught only fleeting glimpses of their great snow peaks, shrouded as these were in almost constant cloud and mist. The thickly vegetated slopes around us however now all seemed formidably steep, with the sheer, moss-covered rock slabs around Mount Speke looking particularly awesome, as they towered up into the mist.

Our ascent up Groundsel Gully to the Elena huts, the climbing base set just below the tip of the Elena Glacier, only a few hundred metres from the site of Abruzzi's original "Ridge Camp", began with another bout of squabbling among our porters (the full complement) over the redistribution of loads outside Cooking Pot Cave.

Once up among the grooved ribs and scree-strewn troughs of rock which mark the approach to the Elena huts, 4,542 m (14,900 ft) above sea level, it is the lowly lichens that prevail, covering the stark, slippery boulders which line the route. Incredibly, while traversing this bleak, glacial landscape, we were "buzzed" by a pair of white-necked ravens (*Corvultur albicolli*), curious custodians of this cold domain.

Setting out the following morning to explore the Stanley Ice Plateau, we were favoured, for a change, with some gloriously clear weather. The views which unfolded were simply breathtaking, compelling us to pause repeatedly on our way up the side of the Elena Glacier, just to look and wonder.

Mount Speke's entire south-western face, dominated by the steep, dipping expanse of the Speke Glacier (the higher parts of which, in hugging the ridge leading up to the summit Vittorio Emanuele, were just tipped by the sun's rays), lay spread before us. So too was the daunting western face of Mount Baker: still unclimbed and in Clive's view "almost certainly the scene of some of the range's stiffest mountaineering challenges".

But for testing climbing propositions we need have looked no further than the steep, eastern faces of Nyabubuya and Kitasamba, the two huge buttresses that guard the Coronation Glacier at the south-eastern edge of Mount Stanley. From the huts both peaks, each scaling roughly 4,860 m (15,945 ft), had looked deceptively close: close enough, anyway, for Clive to scan them for potential new climbing routes.

Two years earlier, with Armand Hughes d'Aeth and Robert Brand, Clive had successfully negotiated a new route up nearby Savoia, the highest of the so-called "Stanley southern peaks". A Grade VI climb involving "mixed" rock, snow and ice work, this route up the peak's rugged north-east ridge had also given Clive his first taste of a tropical snowstorm.

"We must have been a good 150 m (approximately 480 ft) up the ridge when the first clap of thunder rang out," he recalled. "Then, next thing, icy gusts of wind sent shower after shower of spindrift and powder snow cascading down on us.

"Huddled on a narrow belay ledge, we were totally cut off from the world around us by the clouds of billowing spindrift. The pelting must have gone on for a couple of hours, at least."

Looking across now at Savoia, its north-eastern face bathed in sunlight, it was hard to visualise the stormy scene. But the Ruwenzori is renowned for its abrupt weather changes. Clive's mind was still preoccupied with that storm-delayed ascent: with the laying of the runner placements; the difficulties of front-pointing up the ridge's thickly iced notches and grooves, and the niggling business of having to sort out tangled climbing ropes.

"Gaining a niche on ropestretch, we managed," he recounted, "to pull ourselves up onto a sloping snow ramp, from which, through periodic breaks in the cloud, we could see the monolithic Great Tooth down below us, heaped with spectacular rime cornices.

"Soloing up some wider snowfields to the edge of the ridge, we were held up for some time by a huge, overhanging icicle, easily five metres (approximately 15 ft) from top to bottom. After hacking a way around this we suddenly found ourselves well and truly corniced in. A small ice-chimney well over to the right was now our only recourse.

"Conditions then became really precarious," Clive continued. "My crampons were skating about under thigh-deep drifts of mushy snow. Only that 'summit-must-be-just-around-the-corner' feeling drove me on. But it was getting late now, and the fact that the light was going fast was now a big worry.

Mount Baker's daunting north-west face, seen here from the Elena Glacier on Mount Stanley.

The interior of the Elena Hut,
Christmas 1984.

"After scaling a short rock wall (this to avoid having to kick steps up yet another snow ramp), we scrambled finally onto an easy snow slope. A trudge of 100 m (approximately 320 ft) or so over a large snowfield took us up to the true summit: cold and drenched, yes; but we were there at last!"

The descent, Clive later told me, had been something of a mad rush.

"It was getting on for dusk," he said, "when, after two short abseils, we found ourselves crunching across a heavily corniced notch between Savoia and the Great Tooth. The cornices below us were so big that, even in good light, we'd not have been able to see the head of the Elena Glacier. In the gloom, then, we prepared 10 m (approximately 30 ft) of abseil sling and threw the ropes over the edge . . .

"Floating out into space over a mass of bulging cornice, we could feel the abseil ropes slicing deeper and deeper into the lattice-work rime. Landing at the entrance to an ice-cave at the glacier's edge, we hastily coiled our frozen ropes. Then, with our headlamps on, we staggered and slid back down the glacier," he added, "to the small A-frame of the Elena hut."

The clouds closed in on Clive and me with a surprising suddenness while we were on the Stanley Plateau, but not before we had explored, and photographed, some of the fascinating cornice architecture on both Moebius and Alexandra.

Tier upon tier of interlocking crystal forms, whipped up by the wind into fantastic whirls and eddies, now regaled us. And melt-off from the candy-floss-like cornice eaves hung down, refrozen, in long, crystalline curtains of glinting, sword-like icicles. The sweeping plateau, meanwhile, wind-dimpled and gleaming white, seemed to trail off into space.

The next morning saw us crossing the plateau again, this time bound for the

Seasonal melt-down of rime frost on the Stanley Plateau.

great snow pyramid of Margherita: a route which took us, first of all, over the snowy hump at the foot of Alexandra's south-east ridge (the scene of much of our earlier reconnaissance) and down into the dip below the Margherita Glacier.

In climbing the steep snow rise on the other side of this dip, the next stage in proceedings, we skirted some formidable crevasses before finally bashing our way up onto the crest of Margherita's east ridge over thick piles of crumbly rime. Once here, we had little difficulty in following the ridge-line up onto the summit, the highest point on the Ruwenzori Mountains.

Looking across now at Alexandra, it was the dramatic ice-cliffs strung out along the peak's south-eastern ridge, conspicuous enough earlier on our way up, that especially caught our eye. But, with the clouds already creeping in (though it was not yet 11 am), we hurried down off Margherita, to complete the simple traverse that would take us to the top of nearby Albert, via the short snow ridge linking the two peaks.

Mount Stanley's southern peak region: (left to right) Philip, Elizabeth, the Savoia Glacier, and Savoia with (below it) the secluded "snow bowl" of the Coronation Glacier.

(*Opposite*) The Kitandara Lakes bejewel the botanical paradise of the Butawu Valley.

Surprisingly, Albert was among the few major Ruwenzori peaks that eluded the Abruzzi party of 1906. And it was left to the Belgian mountaineer, Count Xavier de Grunne, to conduct the first known ascent of the peak, more than a quarter of a century afterwards in 1932.

The pick-axe whose old-fashioned, forged head Clive had found partially buried on the Albert snow summit in January 1985 could, for all we know, have been left behind here by the de Grunne party. "It was certainly of pre-World War II vintage," Clive maintains, "and, with its handle on, must have weighed at least five kilogrammes."

He had taken it back down with him to the Elena huts, with the intention, he says, of forwarding it somehow to one of the private European collectors of "Ruwenzoribilia". But, sadly, it had mysteriously disappeared "somewhere on the way down to Kitandara".

"I can only think," Clive joked, "that the porters must have quietly jettisoned it, in order to defuse a possible set-to over who was going to have to carry it."

This time, though, Albert produced nothing of great note. And, after rounding off our tour of the "northern Stanley peaks" with an ascent the next morning of Alexandra, we turned our attention again to the southern peaks.

Our aim, specifically, was to explore the Coronation Glacier and its two western peaks, Elizabeth and Philip. At 4,929 m (16,170 ft) and 4,920 m (16,140 ft), these are, respectively, the seventh and eighth highest peaks on the Ruwenzori. Our best access to these peaks, we had agreed, would be from a bivouac sited just below the Savoia Glacier, at the extreme southern end of Mount Stanley.

So, having made our way down the Butawu Valley to the Kitandara huts, where we had linked up again with our porters, we returned to within easy reach of the snows, basing ourselves for the next three days at the foot of a cliff rising from the steep scree slope beneath the glacier. We were now almost directly across from the daunting western cliffs of Mount Baker.

From here we made several trips up the side of the glacier and over the snow col coming down off Nyabubuya onto the Coronation Glacier. The latter, in sweeping down off the col and thence up again to the ice-cliffs on the south face of Savoia peak, is a huge, secluded bowl of snow and ice, all but hidden from view from most other vantage points on Mount Stanley. Tucked away thus, it is little wonder that this dazzling white basin was the central Ruwenzori's last-revealed major topographical feature.

Its "discoverers" were the British mountaineers Arthur Firmin and Douglas Busk who in 1953 established that, far from being merely an extension of the more conspicuous Savoia Glacier (as had previously been supposed), the basin was in fact of wholly independent standing, flanked by two then unnamed peaks. In calling these peaks Elizabeth and Philip, the pair made a lasting tribute to the coronation, that same year, of Britain's Queen Elizabeth II.

Our departure from "the snows which feed the Nile" was followed by a three-day "wind-down" period around the Kitandara Lakes. And, within two more days, we were back at the Nyabitaba hut, having completed the circuit (a complete circumnavigation of Mount Baker) in just four days short of a month.

It is the Kitandara Lakes that, for me, stand out as perhaps the most abiding memory of the entire trip. These lakes are set, for one thing, in the midst of a botanical paradise: a wonderland of giant flora where even the rocky outcrops on the water's edge are "livened up" with colourful mosses and lichens; one species of brilliant orange lichen in particular.

The water, for its part, is continually changing colour with the light: at one moment a steely blue; then a dull, slate grey, and then a pale, emerald-like green. Its stillness, while making it a perfect mirror for the many wonderful views across the lakes (notably those of the jagged peaks of Mount Luigi di Savoia, to the south), can be absolutely deathly.

When combined with the eerie silence of weird lake-shore vegetation, this almost constant stillness creates a haunting atmosphere in which the alarming, or peculiar, seems perpetually poised to happen. And, when a pair of black ducks (*Anas sparsa*) suddenly scoots out from the nearby shallows, the initial reaction is one of fright, as though it were the Loch Ness Monster itself that had appeared.

At such times even the account which Stephen Bagge—an official in Uganda's early colonial administration, who visited the Ruwenzori in 1898— claimed to have heard from his African cook, on the subject of the latter's lone venture up onto the moorlands, does not seem altogether *too* far-fetched. The cook (whose name was not mentioned) is reputed to have spoken of "finding a small lake, on the shores of which were black birds as large as sheep and bellowing like bulls".

(*Opposite*) Evening vista across the
Kitandara Lakes to the jagged peaks
of Mount Luigi di Savoia.

3 · Cave-Riddled Colossus: Mount Elgon

Gordon Boy

Mount Elgon, a huge dormant volcano straddling the Uganda/Kenya border, is far and away the largest of Africa's solitary mountains. Its massive base, in places more than 80 km (approximately 50 miles) across, has led some to speculate that it may once have been Africa's highest mountain. Formed in a series of explosive eruptions, beginning about 24 million years ago and continuing intermittently throughout the Miocene epoch, Elgon's volcanics rest on the Pre-Cambrian bedrock of the Trans Nzoia Plateau like a giant cake on a plate.

The crater on the top of the cake, eaten away by the erosion of centuries, has long since caved in around the edges, leaving an immense, tumbled caldera that on average is nearly eight kilometres (approximately 5 miles) across. Elgon's main peaks, Wagagai, 4,321 m (14,178 ft) above sea level; Sudek, 4,302 m (14,115 ft); Koitobos, 4,222 m (13,852 ft), and Mubiyi, 4,211 m (13,816 ft), are the highest of many weird-looking rock sculptures that lie in a wide ring about the caldera.

Thus eroded, the summit of Elgon is dwarfed by Kilimanjaro, as well as by mounts Kenya and Meru, of Africa's other great solitary mountains. Two of the Virunga volcanoes are higher, as too are peaks on the Ruwenzori and on both the Semien and Bale Ranges in Ethiopia. Elgon, then, for all its great bulk, is now only the eighth highest massif in Africa.

Elgon's last large-scale eruption probably occurred about 10 million years ago and the mountain has apparently not erupted at all for the past three million years. However hot springs still bubble away on the caldera floor, some 600 m (approximately 2,000 ft) below the general level of the caldera rim. Inside the caldera inward rock-falls and landslides have with time created a fascinating, tumbled landscape of rugged steps and tussock-covered hummocks of piled glacial debris and volcanic tuff. One terminal moraine, 150 m (approximately 500 ft) in height, forms a massive, three-kilometre bank along the base of the caldera's inner eastern rim.

The glaciers which in Pleistocene times covered much of the summit of Elgon, reaching down the outer mountain slopes to altitudes of 3,500 m (11,483 ft) or lower, have long since disappeared. In their wake they left behind any number of tiny "rock basin" lakes, many of them in the caldera itself, where they are strung out one below another, paternoster fashion.

Streams from the tiny lakes serve as the catchment of the Suam River, which makes its exit from the caldera via the spectacular Suam Gorge, a deep gash in the eastern caldera wall. Elgon's hot springs, bubbling up at 48 degrees C, are located near the head of this stupendous gorge, itself gouged out of the mountainside over thousands of years by the might of the melting glaciers.

The only other deep breach in the caldera wall is that of the Uganda Pass on

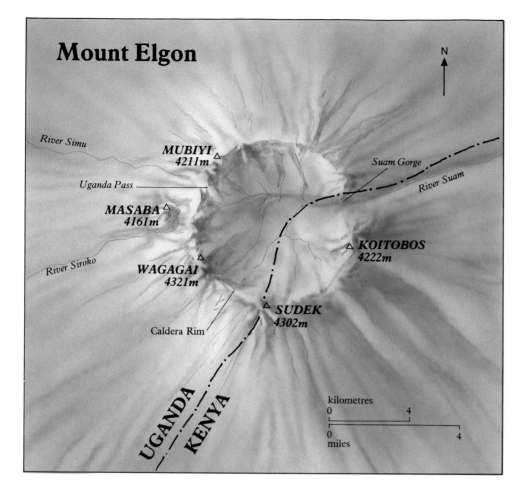

Mount Elgon

the western side, where the River Simu draws its headwaters. Otherwise, the caldera rim, though severely eroded in places, mainly by frost action, is more or less intact, a broad ring of serrated cliffs topped with bold, free-standing pinnacles and crags.

The highest peaks, Wagagai, on the rim's south-western side, Sudek, its far southern edge, Koitobos, well over to the east, and Mubiyi, on the west end of the rim's severed northern arc, are literally kilometres apart. Stretched between them, in the caldera's deep, hilly void, is the realm of some of Elgon's most luxuriant Afro-alpine flora.

Whole forests of the huge endemic tree groundsel *Senecio barbatipes*, thick, spreading boughs cushioned with mosses, cling to the damp, sloping ground, itself covered with a tangled, knee-deep mat of silvery-blue lady's mantle (*Alchemilla spp.*) herbiage. In the dips between hillocks, meanwhile, lie extensive tracts of bogland and swamp, dotted with pale tussocks of *Carex* sedge and bristling with the tall, erect flower spikes of the endemic lobelia, *Lobelia elgonensis*.

So spread out are the Elgon peaks that it seems hard to believe, at first, that they could possibly all rest on the same caldera rim. This, coupled with the fact that no one peak stands markedly higher than its fellows, gives rise to the startling tricks of perspective which so confounded many of the mountain's first European visitors, who, while eager to climb to the "very top" of Elgon, could not determine which of the peaks was indeed *the* top.

Seen from around Mbale, on the western (Ugandan) side of the mountain, the Elgon skyline is dominated by Masaba, a huge, knob-shaped lump of rock which has come to be known latterly as Jackson's Summit. In fact, this knob-like prominence, standing 4,161 m (13,650 ft) above sea level, is not, properly speaking, on the Elgon summit crown at all, being positioned some distance to the west of the caldera, near the head of the upper Siroko Valley.

Masaba is the name of the legendary father of the Bukusu, or Bagisu, tribe of Bantu land tillers who settled in about AD 1500 on the fertile western and south-western foothills of Mount Elgon. Here, they came to view the mountain as their spiritual home, calling it Masaba, whom they saw as being personified by the apparent highest peak. Masaba's wife Wagagai, meanwhile, was embodied in the peak which later proved to be Elgon's highest, but which from most angles looks anything but.

The explorer Henry Morton Stanley wrote of having glimpsed the mountain in 1875, while circumnavigating Lake Victoria during the second of his great central African expeditions. This sighting, almost certainly the first by any white man, is recorded, in Stanley's *Through the Dark Continent* (1878), as "Marsawa".

The mountain's first European visitor was the British geographer and explorer Joseph Thomson, late in 1883. Thomson, who approached the mountain from the Uasin Gishu Plains out to the east, in what was then Maasai territory, wrote of it as "an enormous mass . . . quite comparable to Mount Kenia itself, *without* the snow-clad upper peak".[1]

Thomson's first views of the mountain, like all views from the east on what is now the Kenyan side, would have been dominated by the bold outline of Koitobos peak, the long, flat castle of rock which stands out tall and sheer against the sky, easily the mountain's highest-looking point.

Koitobos, along with Elgon's other major peaks, is, under present global climatic conditions, well below the permanent snow-line. Yet sometimes, looking up at it from the Trans Nzoia Plateau around Kitale, it is covered in the

Across Elgon's caldera, from the head of the Suam Gorge towards Mubiyi peak in Uganda.

(*Opposite*) The Suam Gorge in the east wall of the Elgon caldera.

[1] Thomson, J. J.: *Through Masai Land*; Sampson Low & Co (London), 1885.

Side view of the Makingeny entrance chamber, Mount Elgon National Park.

that formed the mountain. Covered by huge ash-falls, the branches and roots of these ancient fallen trees have, along with the ash itself, been turned to stone.

Sparkling crystals of zeolite (natrolite) and calcite line deep moulds left in the cave-ceilings by ancient, hollowed fossil-logs, while bats hang from the white branches of stone trees more than 10 million years old. In places massed crystals of the secondary mineral salt mirabilite (sodium sulphate or "glauber salts") grow out of the cave-walls in magnificent long curls, like spindly, grey-white ferns.

The walls of the agglomerate caves, rich in such mineral salts, are scored with the tusk-marks of countless generations of elephants. The elephants on Elgon have the unique habit of venturing deep into the ground in order to obtain their vital salt rations. An encounter in the caves with one of Elgon's great animals is a truly unforgettable experience.

The walls are patterned, too, with the scrape- and scrabble-marks of myriads of other feet and teeth, both big and small. For Elgon's extraordinary salt-mining animals, besides elephants, include buffaloes (*Syncerus caffer*), giant forest hogs (*Hylochoerus meinertzhageni*), bushbuck (*Tragelaphus scriptus*), waterbuck (*Kobus defassa*), duikers (*Cephalophus spp.*), monkeys and baboons (*Papio spp.*). The flanks of Elgon are thus riddled with enormous subterranean salt-licks.

Man, too, has left his mark inside the caves. Indeed, many of the Elgon caves were inhabited until well into the twentieth century by Kony and other Sabaot family groups. Some of their cattle- and goat-enclosures and partitions, made from closely woven sticks, are still in place. Pick-marks on the cave-walls show where generations of cave-dwellers and other local tribesmen mined salt for their cattle herds. Many of the cave-ceilings are black with the soot from their torches and fires.

Elgon's caves are most numerous on the lower southern and south-eastern slopes of the mountain, between the 1,800-m (5,900-ft) and 2,500-m (8,200-ft) contours. The largest, and oldest, caves are those found at the lower elevations, in what is now densely populated farming country. Some extend 300 m (approximately 1,000 ft), or more, into the hillsides, and there is one, simply called "the Big Cave", which nobody is yet known to have reached the end of. European settler-farmers, armed with pressure-lamps and trailing rolls of binder-twine behind them, have tried, and failed.

The question of what agency could possibly have created the caves has long been one of Elgon's most engaging mysteries. None of the forces normally associated with cave formation, such as the effects of underground drainage or of wave action, can satisfactorily explain their genesis. Unlike the lava tubes found on some of the other east and central African volcanoes, they are situated not in lava at all, but in agglomerate layers. The theory that they could simply be gas bubbles trapped by lava flows fails to account for their vast dimensions and irregular shapes.

Thomson, whose 1883 visit to Elgon was confined to a brief investigation of the caves, was convinced that they were man-made. The cave-dwellers themselves ridiculed his assumption. Thomson wrote:

> On inquiry . . . I was told that it was God's work. "How," said they, "could we with our puny implements (exhibiting a toy-like axe, their only non-warlike instrument) cut out a hole like this? And this is nothing in comparison with others which you may see all around the mountain. See there, and there, and there! These are of such great size that they penetrate far into utter darkness, and even we have not seen the end of them. In some there are large villages with entire herds of cattle. And yet you ask who made them! They are truly God's work!."[4]

Undeterred by this, Thomson stuck to his view of their artificial origin: "I can come to but one conclusion," he wrote, "and that is, that in a very remote era some very powerful race, considerably advanced in arts and civilisation, excavated these great caves in their search for precious stones or possibly some precious metal."

This view was first challenged in 1897 by C. W. Hobley, then with the IBEA Company but later a provincial commissioner in Kenya. In 1896 he became the first European to make a complete circuit around the massive base of Elgon, a safari which took him just over a month.

Hobley argued[5] that the caves were "undoubtedly due to natural causes", and went on to propound an elaborate theory hinged on the assumption that Lake Victoria, well to the south-west of Elgon, once extended all the way around the mountain. The waters of this great lake, by lapping against Elgon's slopes, he believed, had produced what, in effect, were shoreline caves. What his hypothesis failed to account for was the tremendous altitudinal range over which the caves are found: some occur at altitudes of more than 3,600 m (11,800 ft)!

Many other theories came to light, following the influx in the early 1900s of the region's first white settlers. The Sabaot cave-dwellers, meanwhile, subject to less frequent raids by marauding parties of Maasai and Nandi warriors, began

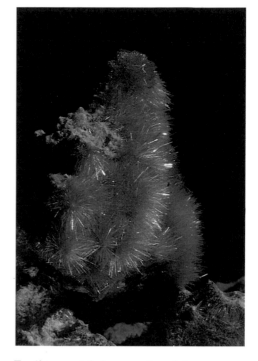

Zeolite crystals have replaced the wood of ancient trees overwhelmed by the volcanism which gave birth to Elgon.

[4] Thomson, J. J. *op. cit.*
[5] Hobley, C. W.: "Notes on a Journey Round Mount Masawa or Elgon"; *Geographical Journal*, Vol. 9 (London), 1897.

(*Following pages*) Koitobos, though not the highest peak on Elgon, dominates views of the mountain from the Kenyan (eastern) side.

gradually to leave their cavernous refuges for a life out in the open.

Sporadic raiding, mainly by the powerful Nandi, continued until very much later, and some Kony groups went on living in their family caves until as recently as the 1960s. They maintained the sturdy barricades of branches and sticks which their forebears had built across the mouths of the caves as a protection against the feared invaders. At night, once all their livestock had been driven inside, a palisade of thick branches would be drawn over the small, centrally positioned entrance.

These fortifications were not always an effective safety shield. One of the Kony people we met in Kitale, Keke Chebus, gave us some harrowing insights into the shortcomings of such a shield. His father, he said, had been the sole survivor of a concerted Nandi onslaught on the Muramoi Cave, home of the Kashiongo sub-clan of the Kony, in 1901. The cave is near the Malikisi River on the southern Elgon slopes.

While laying siege to the cave for three days, the Nandi had succeeded, Keke said, in "putting big piles of dry grass outside the sticks". These, he told us, were then set alight, whereupon "everything caught fire".

"The wind," he said, "took all the smoke inside, and the Kashiongo were forced to the back of the cave. Many of the Nandi who came in first were killed. But they were too many: more than 300, my father said. They started killing everybody with their spears."

Of the 180 cave-dwellers, only Keke's father, then "just a small boy", survived the onslaught: "He was lying down under the bodies," Keke said, "pretending to be dead. There was a big spear wound in his buttocks." The Nandi then "took away all the Kashiongo animals which had not died from the fire: 290 cows and about 40 goats".

Keke, who when we met him was working for an ornithological tour operator based in western Kenya, told us of another Kony sub-clan, the Kapsaitata, who had all perished "not long after", when the roof of their cave-dwelling collapsed, burying them alive. Such were the hazards of cave-life on Mount Elgon.

The completion in 1901 of the Mombasa-Kisumu railway, itself a task that was severely hampered over the final stages by Nandi resistance, brought more and more people, settlers and visitors alike, to western Kenya. A subsequent branch of this "lunatic line", leading north from the Mau Escarpment to Eldoret, then known as Station Sigistifour ("64"), and beyond, further enhanced access by visitors to cave-riddled Mount Elgon.

Among the new wave of visitors to the mountain was the eminent Swiss psychologist Carl Gustav Jung, whose Bugishu Psychological Expedition ("an appellation imposed", Jung himself noted apologetically, "by the Foreign Office in London") traversed Elgon's southern slopes in 1925, following a 70-km (approximately 40-mile) northward trek from Kakamega. "We did visit the Bugishus," he pointed out, "but spent a much longer time with the Elgonyis."[6]

At endless palavers with the tribesmen, Jung continually "brought the conversation around to the numina, especially to rites and ceremonies". He thus recorded what he could of their dreams, fetish objects, rituals, lore and customs. But his greatest illumination, he maintained, was "the discovery of the Horus principle among the Elgonyi" (in ancient Egyptian sun-worship Horus was venerated as the rising sun). The more Jung delved, however, the less assured he began to feel of his own psyche:

"The trip revealed itself," he later stated, "as less an investigation of primitive psychology ('Bugishu Psychological Expedition, B.P.E.'; black let-

---

[6] Jung, C. G.: *Memories, Dreams, Reflections*; Collins/Routledge & Kegan Paul (London), 1963.

Entrance to the Kitum Cave.

ters on the chop-boxes!) than a probing into the rather embarrassing question: what is going to happen to Jung the psychologist in the wilds of Africa?"

The answer, for Jung, then aged 50, seems to have been clear enough: "At that time," he wrote, "I was all too close to 'going back' . . . The only thing I could conclude was that my European personality must under all circumstances be preserved intact." The Elgon of the 1920s was an experience Jung was never to forget, inspiring as it did "warnings", as he called them, "from the unconscious . . . that the primitive was a danger to me".

It was the mystery of the caves, however, which continued to occupy the minds of the majority of Elgon's visitors. Theories of their origin became increasingly complex, invoking among other things a wide variety of chemical reactions.

By the 1960s the most widely accepted explanation was that the caves had been cut by the action of carbonic acid and/or solutions of sulphates and of other corrosive agents present in underground seepages and springs. These chemi-

Makingeny Cave, mined extensively by animals and local tribes.

cals, it was argued, had over the centuries eaten away the calcitic cement from around the agglomerate boulders, precipitating rock-falls which, in turn, had been excavated by man and beast for the salts which they contained, thus producing what in time became considerable caves.

This theory, broadly speaking, still holds sway today, though many feel the rôle played by Elgon's extraordinary salt-mining elephants has been greatly underestimated. Some theorists have gone so far as to suggest that *all* the Elgon caves were excavated, first and foremost, by elephants.

Elephants, like all herbivores on Elgon, depend on geophagy (consumption of mineral-rich earth or rock) for their essential dietary requirements of sodium, magnesium and calcium. These elements are present only in very small concentrations in Elgon's plants since, with an average annual rainfall of nearly 1,300 mm (about 50 inches), the mountain soils are constantly being leached of their soluble mineral salts.

The elephants, unable to lick or nibble the cave-walls like other herbivores, strike the rock with their tusks, gouging off big lumps, which they pick up with their trunks, grind in their mouths and swallow. Their tusks are often noticeably worn down and abraded at the tips from thus being struck against the rock. This, many people now believe, is how most of the Elgon caves came into existence, over many thousands of years.

"The association (of the caves) with waterfalls then becomes clear," writes British wildlife biologist Ian Redmond, who in 1981 made a detailed, nine-week study of one of Elgon's more recent "elephant caves". He argues:

Elephants would be attracted to sites where both mineral-rich rock and water were available. The splashing water would soften the rock, thereby aiding the elephants' efforts, and each generation would learn from its parents the traditional sources of salt.

Despite the mines' extending deeper and deeper into the cliffs, they would continue to be used simply because they had always been used. Rockfalls might block the path, but as long as these were falls of salty rock they too would be eaten.[7]

Kitum Cave, the one studied by Redmond, is one of three caves located within easy reach of the graded dirt road that winds its way upward through the Mount Elgon National Park, a 17,000-ha (approximately 42,000-acre) section of the eastern (Kenyan) side of the mountain. The park, established in the late 1960s, extends from cultivation at 2,100 m (6,890 ft) to the great high castle of weathered rock that is Koitobos peak.

The lower reaches of the park are dominated by the Endebess Bluff, a spectacular wall of lava which for its upper 100 m (approximately 300 ft) or so consists of a vertical cliff-face whose broad, flattish top, 2,570 m (8,430 ft) in altitude, extends back horizontally into the mountainside for several kilometres.

Huge bluffs like this are a characteristic feature of the Elgon slopes, and are especially prevalent on the Ugandan side of the mountain. For Jung, the Endebess Bluff, "*the* bluff" to local, Trans Nzoia farmers, was "a high cliff inhabited by big baboons", the latter reminding him, he wrote, as they gathered on the cliff-edge to await the morning sun, of "the great baboons of the temple of Abu Simbel in Egypt".

The lower forests of the Elgon park around Kitum and Makingeny, two of the best known Elgon caves, are, in places, despairingly dense, comprising dark thickets of wych hazel (*Trichocladus ellipticus*), complete with a rampant undergrowth of spiny acanthus, dark-leaved, holly-like and covered with sticky purple flowers.

These moist forests are alive with animals: giant forest hogs, buffaloes, bushbuck, Harvey's red duikers, bushpigs and, of course, elephants. Black-and-white colobus monkeys, hordes and hordes of them, delight in spectacular leaps about the canopy above, precipitating a more or less constant shower of falling leaves.

The Elgon fauna abounds in species with strong west African affinities. The blue monkey (*Cercopithecus mitis mitis*), for instance, while common in the Elgon forests, does not occur at all on the Aberdares or Mount Kenya, or indeed on any of the great mountains further to the east.

Its range, it seems, was split off millions of years ago from the eastern forests occupied today by its cousins the Sykes' monkeys (*Cercopithecus mitis albogularis*), which do occur on Mount Kenya, by the turmoil surrounding the formation of the Eastern, or Gregory, Rift Valley.

Elgon birds with western affinities include the striking, glossy dark-blue Ross's turaco (*Musophaga rossae*), with yellow face and beak and dashing crimson on its nape and underwings. The black-and-white casqued hornbill (*Bycanistes subcylindricus*) is yet another native of the great central and west African rainforests which has made Elgon its home-from-home.

One of the noisiest of all forest birds, this large, gregarious hornbill has the curious habit on Elgon of nesting, not in holes in trees like the rest of its kind, but in crevices in rocks and lava cliffs. Its whooshing flight and loud, raucous banter resound across the length and breadth of Elgon's forests in the wet, August–September spells, when the fig (*Ficus*) trees are all in fruit.

---

[7] Redmond, I: "Salt-Mining Elephants of Mount Elgon"; *Swara Magazine*, Vol. 5 No. 4 (July/August 1982).

Conyza species, related to groundsel.

Bushbuck skeleton, lodged in a deep crevasse in Makingeny Cave.

The Elgon skies are the province of the crowned hawk-eagle (*Stephanoaëtus coronatus*), most thick-set and powerful of all African birds of prey. A pair of these eagles is a deadly combination: the one, with a riveting display of aerobatic antics, distracts spectating monkeys on the canopy below; the other, swooping bullet-like between the trees, drives home its mighty talons. Monkeys are the birds' main prey, and the ground below an eagle nest, a huge platform of piled sticks high up in a forest tree, is invariably littered with their bones.

The caves, too, are littered with broken bones, chiefly the scattered food debris of leopards and hyaenas, great predators of the Elgon forests, seldom ever seen, but yet always a strongly feared presence.

Deep in a crevasse in a rock-fall near the back of Makingeny Cave lies the complete skeleton of a male bushbuck, its every bone in place. Evidently this hapless creature had fallen while in the cave for its supplement of salt. Unable to climb out of the stony depths, it had perished there. Its skeleton, along with the remains of other casualties, some of them the wedged and partially mummified carcasses of fellow antelopes, is a testimony to the enormous risks which Elgon's salt-mining animals court in the dark.

Near the bushbuck skeleton, feet still locked onto the rock of an overhang in the crevasse, hangs the mummified carcass of a solitary fruit bat (*Rousettus aegyptiacus*), its sinews turned a pale, ghostly green. Preservation of the cave dead has been attributed to a combination of the dry conditions and the abundance of salty mirabilite.

Makingeny, with a huge, domed antechamber and a 30-m (approximately 100-ft) waterfall over its mouth, is the oldest and perhaps the most impressive of the caves in the Mount Elgon park. The chamber floor, more than 70 m (approximately 230 ft) wide, is covered with a fine, powdery dust, in places ankle-deep. Rock-falls from the ceiling have long since been whittled away, or eaten, leaving only the hard, dome-shaped lava cap that now forms the chamber roof.

Elephants still visit Makingeny, but now concentrate their efforts mainly on nearby Kitum Cave. Kitum, though already extending some 170 m (approximately 560 ft) into the mountainside, is still in its infancy, with several new side-chambers still being opened up. The cave-entrance, a low horizontal slit, 50 m (approximately 170 ft) wide, is almost completely blocked by a large rock-fall, through which, however, the elephants have made a narrow trail.

The back of Kitum's main, south chamber is the roosting place of a seething multitude of large tongue-clicking fruit bats. Shine a torch into their midst, and thousands of light-reflecting eyes glow bright red in the beam. Soon the whole cave is filled with a riot of squealing bats. The cacophony is deafening; the heavy

Insectivorous bats massed together on the ceiling of the Makingeny Cave.

air, thick with the stench of guano, is beaten into eddies by the frenzied flapping. Makingeny, by contrast, is favoured by Elgon's diminutive and very much quieter insectivorous bat species.

Perhaps the cave most actively being worked today by elephants is Kirsgek, set higher up the mountainside in dense, secondary bamboo, far from any road and very difficult to find. Kirsgek, which in most respects resembles a smaller, more recent and very much wetter version of Kitum, is also one of Elgon's finest galleries of plant fossils, its roof and walls lined with magnificent stone trees.

Elgon's elephant numbers have been declining dramatically over recent years, falling victim in their hundreds to the depredations of hunters and poachers. Cave-making on Elgon, by elephants at any rate, is thus very much on the wane.

The Elgon slopes outside the park are largely taken up by "forest reserve" plantations of exotic trees, which are fast replacing much of the mountain's indigenous forest. Just outside the park's northern, Kimothon gate, in a rockshelter nestled in a bushy enclave in "forest reserve" territory, rests one of Elgon's greatest enigmas: a frieze of ancient rock paintings depicting wild animals and men with long-horned, northern cattle.

A mummified insectivorous bat still clinging by its claws.

The frieze, first noticed in 1960 by Marjorie Tweedie, a Trans Nzoia-based water-colourist and keen amateur botanist, is considered to be more than 2,000 years old, one of the oldest galleries of rock art in Kenya. Some of the paintings on it are thought to have been done as early as 100 BC. The frieze resolves on close inspection into a haphazard array of semi-naturalistic flatwash animals and human figures, most of them in white, though some are red or red/white bichromes. Only 25 stand out with anything approaching clarity, and even some of these have been irreparably damaged over the past 10 years by thoughtless vandalism.

Stylistically, the paintings show marked similarities to those classed among the "early series" found at Genda-Biftou and at other sites in the Dire Dawa region of Ethiopia. The subject matter alone shows the Elgon frieze to be the work of some far northern culture: the cattle, subjects of most of the paintings, are all long-horned and straight-backed. On none of them can you see the hump of the zebu (*Bos indicus*), the only strain of cattle known in sub-Saharan Africa before historic times.

The inevitable question—who, then, were the artists?—is, and will probably remain, a mystery. The Barabaig, a small pastoralist tribe now ekeing out an existence in the vicinity of Tanzania's Mount Hanang, claim once to have wandered the slopes of Mount Elgon. They were driven off the mountain, they say, by the Kalenjin and the Maasai. Their language, to this day, incorporates

many obvious Kalenjin "borrowings", while their customs reflect a strong Maasai influence.

The Barabaig, though, are of northern, Hamitic stock, and are thought to be descendants of the original "proto-Hamites" who swept southward through Africa about a hundred centuries ago. Theoretically, then, they could have been the Elgon rock-artists. There is however no evidence that any tradition of rock painting has ever existed among them. So the mystery of the Elgon rock paintings, for the time being anyway, lives on . . .

Strange images, hidden at first, materialise one by one out of the rock: non-schematic human figures with bows, sticks, spears maybe, together with domestic cattle, long horns trained (as cattle-horns still are today by northern peoples) into elaborate turns and curves. Out of the rock, too, come animals with branched, or bifurcated, horns like the antlers of deer; a she-dog likeness, and a long-necked evocation of a giraffe. A faint red spiral motif, possibly a sun sign, completes the busy scene, of images being lost and found, lost again and re-revealed.

Elgon's slopes may once have harboured many such images, only to have forsaken them all in the course of centuries of weathering. Geologists have identified Tweedie's Rockshelter as a remnant half-portion of an old phreatic tube, its surface polished smooth by underground water. They maintain it was later shielded from continued erosion by virtue of its dry and secluded position, hemmed in by tall trees.

Such sheltered phreatic channels, according to geologists, are something of a rarity, as regards Elgon's visible volcanic make-up. It is therefore not surprising, they infer, that no other ancient friezes have been discovered on the mountain's weathered slopes.

Back in the Elgon park, a short distance from the Kimothon Gate, a steep track, generally impassable in the late April–May and August–September wet seasons, when it is sometimes a river of mud, winds its way up the side of the Endebess Bluff, through a spectacular scenery of immense *Podocarpus gracilior* trees, said to be among the finest in East Africa. These great trees, some more than 50 m (approximately 160 ft) tall, stand in a sea of bamboo at an altitude of about 2,500 m (approximately 8,200 ft).

From the top of the bluff the track makes the long, steady climb to a roadhead about 3,350 m (11,000 ft) up, passing first through dark, hushed woods of Elgon olive (*Olea welwitschii*) trees and dense roadside clumps of wild elderberry (*Sambucus africana*), before striking out across the wide, sweeping Elgon moorlands, with their scattered hagenia trees, St John's worts and thickets of giant heather.

The Elgon caldera is a stiff, three- to four-hour walk from the roadhead. For much of the way the path keeps to the icy main headstream of the Kimothon River which, a long way down the mountain below the northern park gate, becomes the Koitobos, one of the Trans Nzoia's principal rivers.

Delicate sub-Alpine wild flowers line the lower stretches of the "Kimothon trail", none more striking than the delphiniums (*Delphinium macrocentron*), which seem continually to be changing colour with the light, vacillating between a deep blue and a turquoise-green. Soon the everlastings come into their own, in bright clusters of pink and white.

The valley, steep and V-shaped lower down and bounded by fantastic sculptures of perched rocks, broadens noticeably as the huge, looming bulk of Koitobos, flat but for a deep notch near its southern end, draws closer. Signs of former glaciation become more evident, both in the valley's flatter, U-shaped upper profile and in the accompanying series of recessional moraines, which mark the stages in the ice-cap's long retreat.

This is the cold world now of Elgon's crop of the strange Afro-alpine flora.

Delphiniums flourish in the wetter areas on Mount Elgon.

Giant groundsels (including, in *Senecio elgonensis*, a second endemic species) and lobelias with shaggy, silvery-blue flower spikes (*Lobelia telekii*) retain their dead leaves in protective coats which insulate their stems against the cutting winds and biting sub-zero night temperatures. Augur buzzards (*Buteo rufofuscus*), true mountain raptors, circle overhead, in skies patrolled sometimes by lordly lammergeiers (*Gypaetus barbatus*).

Now the most popular means of access to the caldera, the "Kimothon trail" is just one of many possible routes. From the Kenya side the other main approach is via the Kimilili Track and Laboot, on the southern Elgon slopes. This "Sudek route" has the attraction of affording ready access, too, to the Sudek Tarn, largest and most picturesque of Elgon's "rock basin" lakes which is fringed by tall tree groundsels.

Routes from the Uganda side, once the most trodden of all paths used by visiting hiking parties, have been neglected in recent years, following the demise of the Mountain Club of Uganda (MCU) in the 1970s. In its heyday, this club had established rest-huts on the most popular Ugandan route, that starting out from Bumagabula, 40 km (approximately 25 miles) east of Mbale.

One of the MCU facilities, known as the Ladkin Hut, was positioned in the caldera itself. Vandalised repeatedly in the early 1960s, this hut was finally destroyed altogether, allegedly by zealots of the bizarre and controversial religious cult Dini ya Musambwa, the so-called "religion of ancestral spirits" which sprung up around Mount Elgon in the mid-1940s.

The cult grew up around the teachings of a charismatic, self-styled Luhya messiah named Elijah Masinde. The Musambwa laws, Masinde always claimed, were set down in "a black book, hidden in a cave at the top of Mount Elgon". He alone was authorised, he said, by the Musambwa god, Were, to propagate these laws. This he did at prayer meetings held at secret shrines on the slopes of the mountain.

Central to the Dini ya Musambwa credo was an abhorrence of all things European, a fanatical and often violent anti-establishment activism, and a belief that material wealth "like cars, tractors, clothes . . ." would come to acolytes "from out of the mountain". Mount Elgon came to be known by the sect as "Sayoni": a corruption of the "Zion" of Hebrew religious worship. As Sayoni, Elgon was—indeed is still—revered as the hallowed seat of Were.

Banned in Kenya in its early years by the colonial authorities, the cult has since also been declared illegal by the government of independent Kenya. Even so, Dini ya Musambwa has a clandestine following in both western Kenya and eastern Uganda which still numbers ten of thousands of people.

Masinde himself, interviewed[8] shortly before his death in 1987, at the age of "around 80", recalled how it all began:

One night in April, 1943, God appeared to me while I slept with the words: "I am your God Were of Musambwa spirit. I speak from Sayoni on the consecrated Mount Elgon. I have appointed you, Masinde, to be the leader of Dini ya Musambwa.

"Inform all Bukusu people to believe in the spirit of Musambwa. They will have food in abundance. Tell Musambwa followers not to wear the clothes of Europeans; they should dress instead in the skins of monkeys. I shall cure the deaf and the blind and the crippled. You must hate the Europeans.

"At the end of the world, I, the Almighty God Were of Mount Elgon, shall open a door for you, Masinde. Then you, with all who embrace the holy Musambwa spirit, will enter heaven."

Verreaux's eagle slipstreaming an adult lammergeier.

---

[8] (by) *Drum Magazine* (East); December, 1986.

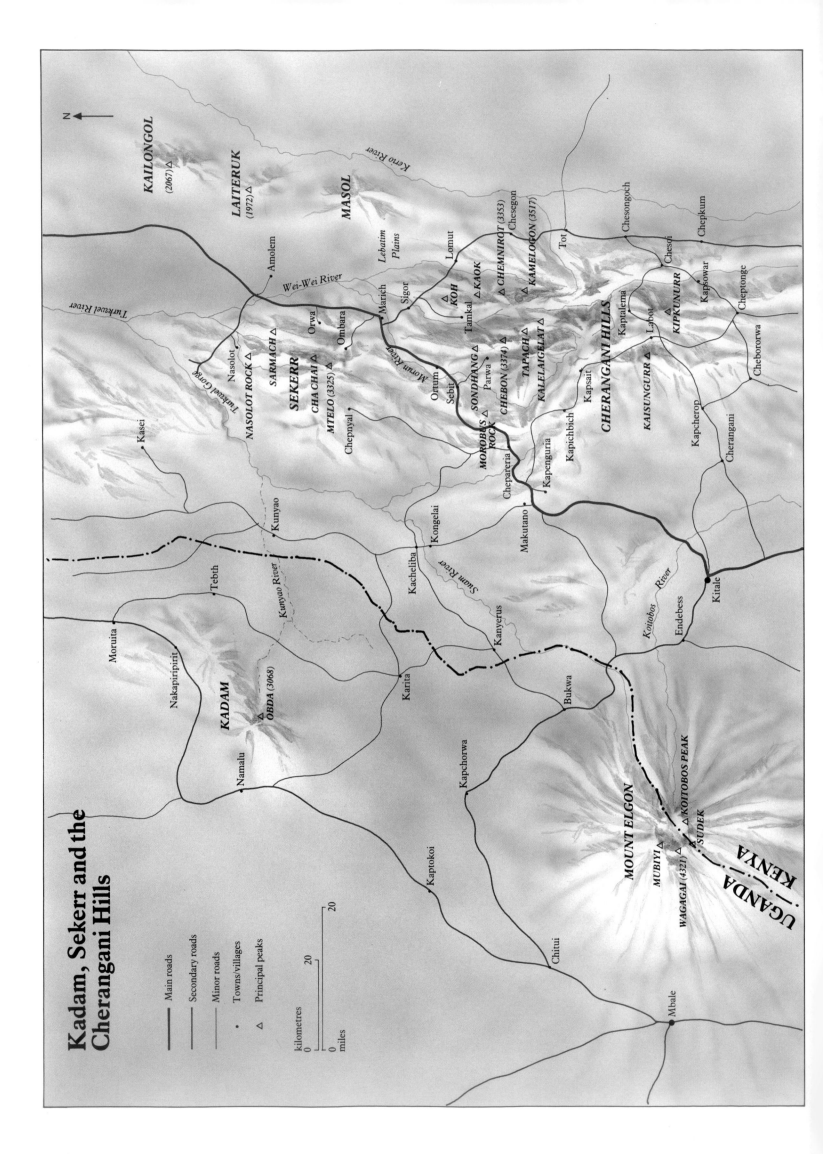

Kadam, Sekerr and the Cherangani Hills

N ←

Main roads
Secondary roads
Minor roads
• Towns/villages
△ Principal peaks

kilometres
0   20
miles
0   20

KAILONGOL (2067)△

LAITERUK (1972)△

MASOL

Kerio River

Lebatim Plains

Amolem

Wei-Wei River

Turkwel River

Sigor

Marich

Lomut

CHEMNIROT (3353)
Chesegon

KAMELOGON (3517)

Tot

Chesongoch

Chesqi

Chepkum

KAOK △

KOH △

Tamkal

Cheptonge

Kapsowar
Kapsowar

KIPKUNURR △

SARMACH △
Orwa
Ombara

Nasolot

NASOLOT ROCK △

SEKERR
CHA CHAI △
MTELO (3325) △

Chepnyal

Ortum
Sebit

Morun River

SONDHANG △
Parwa

CHEBON (3374) △

TAPACH △
KALELAIGELAT △

CHERANGANI HILLS

Kaptalema

Labot

KAISUNGURR △

Kapsait

Kapenguria

Kapichbich

Kapcherop

Cherangani

Chebororwa

Kasei

Turkwel Gorge

MOROBUS ROCK △

Chepareria

Makutano

Kunyao

Kunyao River

Kongelai

Swam River

Kacheliba

Kanyerus

Tebth

Moruita

Nakapiripirit

KADAM
OBDA (3068) △

Namalu

Karita

Kaptokoi

Kapchorwa

Bukwa

Koitobos River

Endebess

Kitale

Chitui

MOUNT ELGON

MUBIYI △

KOITOBOS PEAK △
SUDEK

WAGAGAI (4321) △

UGANDA
KENYA

Mbale

4 · Tenanted Mountaintops: Kadam, Sekerr and the Cherangani Hills

Gordon Boy

"Its cliffs and precipices look inaccessible; yet perched on the very top of them are the dwellings of a people whose language and habits differ considerably from those of the surrounding tribes."

So wrote protestant missionary John Bremner Purvis in describing solitary Mount Kadam, which he saw in 1902 while on a journey across Uganda to Mount Elgon.[1]

"This people," he wrote, ". . . are to be met with again on Mount Moroto, in the north, and since they are undoubtedly of Bantu stock, their presence so far north, and surrounded as they are by powerful Nilotic peoples by whom they are respected, is a striking phenomenon."

Just how and when the Kadamas and the Tepes, as the isolated communities on Kadam and Moroto are known, came to occupy their respective mountain haunts seems likely to remain a mystery. For, although their huts, granaries and *shambas* can still be seen on these mountains today, the people have lost much of their cultural identity, and their mother tongue is now all but forgotten. They have espoused instead the languages and customs of their Nilo-Hamitic neighbours, the Karamojong and the Pokot. And, like these wandering herdsmen of the hot, dry plains around the mountains, many of them, though traditionally land-tillers, have adopted a pastoral way of life. Such a meeting and mingling of different cultures has long been the story of all the diverse mountains out to the north-east of Mount Elgon, near the common border of Uganda and Kenya.

All these mountains, from Kadam and Moroto in far eastern Uganda to the Pokot (formerly Karasuk) Hills, Sekerr and the Cherangani Hills in western Kenya, boast a long history of human habitation. On the tops of some of them rest enigmatic reminders of cultures that have long since disappeared. All are remarkable today for the variety of different peoples and lifestyles they support.

Kadam, 70 km (approximately 45 miles) north of Mount Elgon, is set apart, geologically as well as physically, from the rest of these mountains in being of volcanic origin. Its two main peaks, Obda and Tebtho, are the weathered remnants of lava banks built up millions of years ago around twin vents, both long since extinct. They stand nearly 20 km (approximately 12 miles) apart at opposite ends of a long basalt plateau, with Obda, the higher of the two, rising to 3,068 m (10,067 ft) above sea level.

Kadam and Moroto, a further 75 km (approximately 47 miles) to the north, are two of the most remote and least known of all the great East and Central

---

[1] Purvis Rev. J. B.: *Through Uganda to Mount Elgon*; T. Fisher Unwin (London), 1909.

Cultivation on the summit plateau of Sekerr. These steep *shambas* are tilled by the Masopot ("mountain-dwelling") branch of the Pokot tribe.

African massifs. Skirting the jumble of bluffs on the shoulder of Mount Elgon from Mbale on the Uganda side, the road to Kadam becomes little more than a thin, ribbon-like strip of gravel, threading its way across a flat, arid wilderness of thorny scrub. Here, nomadic Karamojong herdsmen, naked but for their short calico togas or blanket "wraps", step nonchalantly off the road to avoid the long, hovering trail of dust.

The other main approach, from Makutano on the Kenya side via Kacheliba, is much the same, except that it is Pokot pastoralists who make up the bulk of the traffic. Either way, Kadam—or Debasien as it is sometimes called—is at once both dramatic and inspiring, from the moment its sharp, jagged crest-line bursts into prominence on the horizon, boldly silhouetted in deep blue across the vast, shimmering expanse of Uganda's southern Karamoja plains.

It was this prospect that prompted naturalist, painter and explorer Sir Harry Johnston, Britain's special commissioner in Uganda between 1899 and 1905, to declare in his tome *The Uganda Protectorate* (1902) that ". . . so far as outline goes, I think Debasien is the most beautiful mountain in central Africa".

At closer quarters, its heights resolve into a formidable array of sheer lava cliffs, many of them flanked by savage-looking pinnacles and crags. Amid the tumbled rocks and scattered pockets of vegetation at the bases of these cliffs the summit plateau falls away abruptly, in a series of sharp, forest-covered ridges to the level of the surrounding plain more than 1,500 m (approximately 5,000 ft) below. Anticipation builds as, one after another, the many startling forms break out of the hazy blue smoothness of the mountain wall. Getting there is an integral part of Kadam's appeal.

Nestled against the mountain's northern flank lies the small village of Nakapiripirit, with its nearby Catholic mission and, alongside this, an old, sprawling Sudanese refugee camp. Tebtho's spectacular crown of needle-sharp teeth, perched high above the village, makes for a commanding backdrop. The stock trails which zigzag up the mountainside behind the village offer the most ready access to the summit plateau. Even so, the steep trudge up to the base of Tebtho's mighty teeth is a strenuous, five- to six-hour undertaking.

The dense, tangled thickets of acacia near the foot of the mountain soon give way to a more open, grassy cover, cleared in places to accommodate Kadamas *shambas* and settlements. To promote fresh grazing the higher reaches of this zone are regularly burned, generally in February before the onset of the March–May seasonal rains.

The rains, when they come, do so with a vengeance. The year's entire rainfall is often concentrated in just a few heavy downpours. For the rest of the year Kadam is astonishingly dry and there are few permanent streams of any note. At times the only water to be had on the mountain is seepage that collects in tepid puddles or "water-holes" tucked away in recesses between rocks. Few and far between, these puddles, though well known to the locals, are not always easy to find.

Kadam's cool forest belt, encountered at about 2,100 m (approximately 7,000 ft), boasts open stands of olive (*Olea africana*) woodland in its lower reaches, giving way higher up to denser pockets of African beechwood (*Faurea saligna*) and other tall, shade trees. But perhaps the most interesting, and cherished,

Obda, seen here from Tebtho Peak in the north-east, is the highpoint of Uganda's Mount Kadam.

Tebtho's bold "crown of teeth",
mounted on impressive parti-coloured
walls of rock.

tree found on the mountain is *Catha edulis*, better known simply as *miraa*.

Prized as a powerful narcotic stimulant, *miraa* shoots are chewed throughout East and Central Africa. Their reddish outer peel contains strong alkaloids which affect the central nervous system, inducing a state of wakefulness, accompanied by a "high" of mental well-being and alertness. Taken over long periods, they cause a deterioration of the senses, which can lead to insanity, followed by coma and death.

Indigenous to large parts of Africa, *miraa* has long been the continent's most widely taken drug; its earliest recorded names being Qat and "Abyssinian tea". Over much of its range it is little more than a small shrub, but on Kadam it forms tall, graceful trees. The Kadamas and the Karamojong, who chew the twigs constantly (without apparently showing any of the harmful side-effects), call it *emurungi* or *marungi*.

Above the forest-line, thick *Protea* scrub and montane savannah come into their own, mingling on the summit plateau with dense thickets of giant heather. The resulting tangle makes the going slow and awkward, calling for the use of a *panga* in places, to chop a way through the obstructing foliage.

The peaks, facing each other across the wide, slanting plateau, are like the ruined castles of rival fairytale kingdoms; embodiments of two wholly different architectural styles. Tebtho's upstacked needles, seen from closer up, become huge, fluted columns, rearing up like giant organ pipes. Obda, off to the south-west, is a massive, smooth-walled tower. Its stupendous flanks, sheer cliffs hundreds of metres in height, culminate in a flat expanse of barren table-land. Obda, with comparatively few sharp angles or projecting crenellations or turrets, belongs (it would seem) to the older of Kadam's two spent volcanoes, since erosion has long since smoothed its sides.

Both peaks are girdled in well-nigh impenetrable heather, and from the plateau the ascent of either may take several hours. Between the two stands Natenus, an isolated lava plug that looks just like a monumental sculpture of a tribal drum.

Out to the north of Kadam, across the grassy plains, the rounded hump of Moroto Mountain can just be seen. It is astonishing to think that, not a hundred years ago, the country between these two mountains was literally teeming with big game. It was here, in the late 1890s, that Scotsman Walter "Karamoja" Bell, the first white man to venture into the heart of the region, earned himself the reputation as the greatest of all the early elephant hunters. Just a short distance north of Kadam, Bell wrote of coming "face to face with such a gathering of elephant as I had never dared to dream of even. The whole country was black with them, and what lay beyond them one could not see as the country was dead flat."[2]

Today these great elephant herds are no more. And gone too are the equally astounding populations of rhinos and other animals that Bell encountered. Otherwise southern Karamoja remains just as wild and ungovernable now as it was at the turn of the century. Since the 1970s both Moroto and Kadam have served, off and on, as strongholds for armed rebel insurgents loyal to past, toppled Ugandan regimes. In speaking of the rebels the local people, it seems, all favour the same image: "These warriors," they say, "have sub-machine guns for walking-sticks."

Moroto, marginally higher than Kadam at 3,083 m (10,116 ft) above sea level, is an altogether different *kind* of mountain in that it is not a product of volcanic activity. It is in fact composed of very much more ancient basement complex rocks. Regarded as the northern outpost of the Kenya–Tanzania highlands, Moroto is the detached end portion of a long, broken mountain chain strung out on a weathered fault-line scarp along the western margin of the Eastern, or Gregory, Rift Valley. The chain, picking up south-east of Moroto, curves away to the south, across the western frontier region of Kenya. It takes in the many striking peaks of the remote Pokot Hills, before linking up eventually with Sekerr and, finally, with the sprawling Cherangani Hills, more than 160 km (approximately 100 miles) distant.

The highest peaks on the Pokot Hills are Kachagalau and Lorosuk, at 2,791 m (9,156 ft) and 2,786 m (9,140 ft) respectively. But several other points on the

[2] Bell W. D. M.: *The Wanderings of an Elephant Hunter*; Country Life Library (London), 1923.

The rolling plateau moorlands of the high Cherangani are subject to nightly frosts and biting winds.

Panning for gold in the Nasolot River.

mythical home of Elat, traditional rain god of the Pokot. Subordinate only to Tororut, the supreme god of Pokot mythology, Elat is also lord of death. The dread he inspires, in this capacity, is such that the beautiful pools of Tomogir have long been carefully avoided by the Pokot, for fear of being sucked into the murky depths, never to return.

Tororut, the giver of all life, is said to have appeared long ago, before some of the earliest Pokot forebears, as a giant-like figure with huge, outspread wings, the latter corresponding to the heavenly vault of the sky. Mtelo, the summit of Sekerr, 3,325 m (10,910 ft) above sea level, is reputed to be Tororut's chosen resting place and vantage point, and is revered accordingly. For centuries Pokot dead have been buried facing it. Likewise, important tribal rites and ceremonies, such as the *sapana* following circumcision, have traditionally been performed facing Mtelo. "Mtelo!", moreover, is frequently invoked in conversation to stress the veracity of a statement or claim and is the rough equivalent of an expression like "Gospel truth!".

Farmers, too, from as far afield as Mount Elgon, habitually keep a watchful eye on Mtelo in the hot, dry months. A prolonged build-up of thick cloud on

Sekerr, they say, is always a sure sign that the long, soaking rains are on the way, and is the signal for them to start planting their crops.

The ascent of Mtelo is no small undertaking. From Orwa, a little speck of a village nestled among shady trees at the eastern foot of Sekerr, it took us all of eight hours to get to the base of the sacred mound, and a further two, the next morning, to scramble up onto the summit.

There are, of course, other ways of getting there. A long, tortuous track winding up the mountainside from Marich, in the south, leads eventually to the high-lying settlement of Mbara, with its Lutheran mission and adjacent school buildings. When passable (and then only to four-wheel-drive vehicles), this "road" makes it possible to avoid the first, and steepest, part of the climb.

This initial steep part over, the route crosses a vast, undulating central plateau, bristling with tall, candelabrum-shaped *Euphorbia* trees. The plateau, with Sekerr's main peaks disposed in a large circle around it, seems totally removed from the world below; hemmed in by Mtelo, Chorwa and Chachai in the north, Kangatip in the west, Cheptem and Motong in the east and Sewera and Koghmot in the south.

For a hundred years or more, this remote plateau has been the domain of increasing numbers of land-tilling Pokot, known collectively as *Masopot* (literally "mountain-dwellers") by their pastoralist kin on the surrounding plains. Their *shambas*, under maize, mainly, or finger millet, hug the higher ground about the plateau's edge, some of it precariously steep.

Above the level of this cultivation what mountain paths there are soon peter out, amid thick *Protea* brush and wiry bracken. Then comes a broad belt of dense montane forest, complete with magnificent *Olea* and *Podocarpus* trees, many of them festooned with orchids and lichens.

Next there is a jungle of thick bamboo, and, above this, a delightful belt of "elfin forest", with lush, mossy glades and clusters of the tall "forest lobelia", *Lobelia gibberoa*. The summit itself, Tororut's gently rounded perch, is covered with giant heather and open, tussock grassland.

These vegetation zones, though typical of all Africa's tropical mountains, are perhaps more compressed, more sharply defined, here than on most other mountains. It is possible, on Mtelo, to pass through all the main sub-Alpine plant zones, from thornscrub-savannah to moorland, in a mere couple of hours.

Buffaloes are still very much in evidence around Mtelo; their fresh trails in places offering the only practical way through the tangled undergrowth of brambles and nettles in the forest, or through the close-set bamboo. Signs of bushbuck and giant forest hog can also still be seen, and leopards (*Panthera pardus*) are still reported, now and then, to take goats on the plateau below.

For all its great size, Sekerr is really just a small part of the far larger Cherangani range, to the south of it, split off, as though from its parent massif, by the deep cleft of the Marich Pass.

Carved through the mountains by the Morun River in forcing its way northward after tumbling down off the high, rolling moorlands of the Cherangani Hills, the pass is a major thoroughfare for traffic using the "great north road" linking Kenya with the Sudan. The journey through the pass from Marich and up the steep Kamatira Escarpment on the Cherangani's north-western flank to Kapenguria, administrative capital of Kenya's West Pokot district, must rate as one of the country's most scenic mountain drives. Tarred since 1983, the twisting, turning road hugs the steep sides of the pass, criss-crossing the lower Morun Valley.

The river, sometimes far below the road, is lined with the scattered debris of uprooted trees, a testimony to the force with which the water must come rushing down in the rainy months. It was on this stretch of the Morun, among the river's big white boulders, that gold-panning really began in West Pokot, in

The gloryosa, which flourishes on the dry, eastern slopes of the Cherangani.

(*Following pages*) The Sondhang Ridge, northerly arm of the Cherangani Range, from a viewpoint near Morobus, in the west.

the 1940s. Thriving settlements, such as those at Wakor and around Ortum, have since grown up around this search for "river gold".

Higher up, where the valley flattens out, it is acacias, aloes, cactus-like *Euphorbia* trees and fleshy, blue-green milkweed (*Calotropis procera*) shrubs that line the route, along with any number of tall, red termite mounds and spires. The great, frowning cliffs of the Cherangani's northward-tending Sondhang Ridge make for an impressive backdrop. These cliffs are said to harbour Kenya's largest single colony of lammergeiers or bearded vultures.

Branching off the tarmac at the top of the Kamatira Escarpment, high above the prominent, outlying sentinel of Morobus Rock, is the "Cherangani Highway", a dirt track leading via the ridgetop settlements of Kapichbich and Kapsait into the heart of the high Cherangani. Often impassable in the wet months, the "highway" owes its rather grand name to the European settlers who built it in the early 1940s, to enhance the sheep farming potential of the western Cherangani highlands.

The headwaters of the Morun, just a short distance from Kapsait, offer some of the finest trout fishing to be had in Kenya, if only because the setting, described by Johnston, in *The Uganda Protectorate*, as "swelling green downs crested with beautiful woodland", is so exhilarating and tranquil.

The sameness of the terrain can be unnerving, though. Fishing the Morun as a child, I remember being scared, as only a child can, by the fact that I could follow the river all day and yet, it seemed, always be surrounded by identical moorland hummocks and vales. There were times when the only sense of direction lay in the flow of the river itself. Devoid of distinctive landmarks, the Cherangani skyline can play havoc with the sense of distance.

With no fewer than six groups of summits rising to more than 3,200 m (10,500 ft) above sea level, the Cherangani is hardly a range of mere "hills". Yet, were it not for their great altitude, these summits could quite easily be taken for stretches of downland in say Scotland or Wales.

The absence of dramatic peaks and of rugged or startling forms betrays the great age of the massif. Its ridge-lines, once sharp and jagged, have been weathered down and smoothed by time. They are made up largely of quartzites and gneisses: ancient metamorphic rocks uncovered on the earth's surface by hundreds of millions of years of erosion.

Giant heather on Chemnirot catches the evening light as the clouds mass over the Cherangani.

On parts of the Cherangani, as on Sekerr, the erosion process has laid bare a still older core of igneous granite. Intrusion of this granite, in its original, molten state, into the overlying strata is thought to have occurred more than 2,000 million years ago. The Cherangani's varied mineral wealth, including as this does deposits of gold, copper, graphite, nickel, kyanite and chromium, dates from this time. The minerals, trapped as liquids or gases in the molten granite, escaped into existing cavities and cracks in the surrounding rock, and were deposited as ore veins.

None of the veins is considered workable on a large, industrial scale, and mining, though much in evidence on the lower Cherangani slopes, rests solely in the hands of small-scale operators. The same holds true for gemstones, which occur in scattered pockets in the range's metamorphic rock. Sapphires, rubies and garnets (including crystals of deep-red spessartite) are all found on the Cherangani.

The range's higher summits, Kamelogon, at 3,517 m (11,540 ft); Chebon, 3,375 m (11,073 ft); Chemnirot, 3,353 m (11,000 ft); Kalelaigelat, 3,350 m (10,991 ft); Tapach, 3,296 m (10,814 ft), and Sondhang, 3,207 m (10,520 ft) above sea level, are perched like rows of knuckles atop parallel north-south ridges, running like a double-wall along the west Rift margin.

More than 60 km (approximately 35 miles) long, these mountain walls are intersected by a third, and probably very much older, quartzite ridge, which

curves in from the west, being an extension of the Kamatira Escarpment. The resulting basic structure of the range is that of a massive, raised "H".

All the main summits on the western arm of the "H" are readily accessible from the "Sondhang Road", a rutted cul-de-sac veering northward from the mountain settlement of Kapsangar, itself linked to the "Cherangani Highway" by a track cutting across the upper Morun Valley from Kapsait. Kalelaigelat, Tapach, Chebon and Sondhang all lie within easy reach of this "road".

The traverse from the Sondhang Ridge, across the "bridge" of the "H", to Kamelogon, the highest point on the Cherangani Hills, involves four hours, or more, of hard walking, complete with many steep ups and downs, over and through a labyrinth of subsidiary ridges and valleys.

The "woodland crests" referred to by Johnston are dominated, here as elsewhere on the Cherangani, by exceptionally tall stands of giant heather, St John's wort and a huge, endemic tree groundsel (*Senecio cheranganiensis*). The presence of this groundsel bears witness to the long isolation of the range even from nearby Mount Elgon, 80 km (approximately 50 miles) away to the west.

The rolling, open downland, for its part, is decked with a variety of montane flowers. Coral-red blooms of the rare ground orchid *Disa starisii* peep out between grassy tussocks, as too do delicate mauve bells of the iris (*Dierama pendulum*), held aloft on fine, thread-like stalks. White flower spikes of the hardy foxglove (*Hebenstretia dentata*) line paths studded with brilliant yellow *Haplocarpha* flowers, spread flat on the ground as though pressed.

North or south, as far as the eye can see, the undulating pasture-land is dotted with the thatched round huts, and lined with the split-bamboo sheep pens, of the Cherangani's resident Pokot and Elgeyo–Marakwet shepherds. The range's

Undulating pasture land in Elgeyo-Marakwet territory, south of Kamelogon. These pastures are dotted with the thatched hut-dwellings of the Cherangani shepherds.

central "bridge-land" forms part of the boundary dividing these two related, yet fiercely independent, tribes.

Falling away on both sides through a series of steep, bamboo-covered spurs, the "bridge-land" forms the head, too, of the range's two most spectacular, and secluded, valleys: the Mwina, to the north, and the Arror to the south.

Despite tumbling down in opposite directions, the Mwina and the Arror rivers both ultimately contribute to the drainage bound for Lake Turkana. Becoming the Wei-Wei on reaching the Lebatim Plains and being joined there by the Morun, the Mwina drains into the Turkwel; while the Arror, flowing a long way south, is eventually channeled northward on joining the Kerio River. By contrast, streams arising on the range's south-western slopes, all flow, via the Nzoia River, to Lake Victoria. The Cherangani watershed thus represents a major divide between the Turkana and the Victoria-Nile drainage.

Nestled in the upper reaches of the Mwina and the Arror valleys are the last remaining substantial portions of the Cherangani's once-vast montane forest. The rest, sadly, has largely been cleared, with the advance of cultivation up the slopes. These forests possibly still harbour small, remnant herds of the rare eastern bongo (*Boocercus eurycerus isaaci*), the largest and most magnificent of all forest antelopes, having dark chestnut-coloured flanks "sliced" vertically with brilliant white stripes.

Once common on the Cherangani, the elusive bongo, seldom ever seen, even on the Aberdare Mountains, its one remaining major sanctuary, is widely presumed to have been exterminated from these "hills". But one of our Pokot guides, Loshang'ura Long'oris, who has lived at the edge of the Mwina Forest all his life, assured us that he still "sometimes finds the spoor" of the animal in the dense forest and bamboo at the valley head. Interestingly, there is no record of the bongo's ever having occurred in the forests of Mount Elgon, which is another pointer to the long separation of the two land-masses.

A precariously steep path down the northern tip of Korochok, a rugged spur jutting out into the Mwina Valley from the Nokughen rock promontory at the base of Kamelogon, is the lifeline for the Pokot shepherds who live on this, the highest part of the Cherangani range. Week after week, these mountain-dwellers make the steep journey down to the Tamkal market on the banks of the Mwina River and back up again with their donkeys; the latter returning laden with sacks of grain and other essential provisions. The whole journey takes the best part of two days; the ascent, alone, from Tamkal to the top of Kamelogon, took us more than ten hours.

It is high enough, here, to be bitterly cold, particularly at night, when temperatures drop to below Zero Centigrade, leaving a heavy frost to be crunched underfoot in the early mornings.

Looking north from Kamelogon, over the rounded peaks of Chemnirot and Kaok, along the Cherangani's eastern wall, the view is dominated by the spectacular form of Koh, easily the range's most dramatic single feature. Crowned with a smooth rock dome, Koh, though no more than 2,750 m (about 9,020 ft) above sea level, looks imposing even from as far away as Mtelo, on Sekerr. Towering above the village of Sigor and accessible from the Sigor–Tamkal road, Koh itself affords magnificent views out across the Lebatim Plains.

East of Kamelogon, the wall drops away sharply, through a succession of near-vertical spurs and precipices, to the Rift floor, more than 2,000 m (approximately 6,500 ft) below the summits, in one of the highest and perhaps the most spectacular of all the great escarpments that bound the Great Rift Valley.

The views out over the Rift from the edge of the Tot, or Elgeyo, Escarpment, as this is called, are simply breathtaking. Rising from the middle of the gaping

Elgeyo-Marakwet goatherd on one of Kaisungurr's mysterious Sirikwa burial mounds, on the southern Cherangani highlands.

chasm, here more than 100 km (approximately 60 miles) wide, is the long spine of the Tugen, or Kamasia, Hills which separate the deep trough of the Kerio Valley from the Rift floor proper. Just north of the Tugen Hills stands the lone volcanic peak of Tiati, held sacred by the native Tugen people.

The Cherangani, left stranded in the wake of the Rift Valley's collapse, is the highest-standing remnant of an ancient plateau that once covered much of west and central Kenya. The plateau's origins have been traced back to sediments laid down thousands of millions of years ago, in what geologists believe must once have been a vast lowland basin extending north-south along the margin of a former African sub-continent. These sediments, buried and so subjected to increased pressures and temperatures, were later gradually metamorphosed.

Then, about 30 million years ago, the whole plateau was domed upward, along the site of the present-day Rift Valley, by immense forces that came into play underneath the earth's surface. The same forces caused the sagging of the plateau in the west, and the formation there of the Lake Victoria Basin. Ensuing episodes of violent down-faulting opened up huge cracks along the crest of the dome, which then collapsed, in several stages, to form the Rift Valley as we know it today. The dome, judging from the steep, 60- or 70-degree angles at which some of the strata on the Cherangani lie, must have attained a prodigious height; just how high we shall never know.

The highest intact portion of the so-called "Kenya Dome", the Cherangani is considered to be unique among Africa's higher mountains in being a residual, as

Karamojong grandmother on Kadam. In keeping with ancient custom, she wears a lip plug.

opposed to an up-faulted or a fold-type, crystalline massif. Its corresponding western "half", on the opposite side of the rift, is the very much lower Leroghi Plateau, in Samburu territory, well to the east of the Tugen Hills.

Some way south of Kamelogon, in the heart of what is now Elgeyo–Marakwet territory, there are enigmatic reminders of an advanced African culture that has long since disappeared, that of the mysterious Sirikwa people, the range's probable first tenants.

The entire eastern face of Kaisungurr, 3,161 m (10,391 ft) high and one of the Cherangani's two southern markers (the other being the slightly lower mass of Kipkunurr), is an old Sirikwa graveyard, dotted with commemorative mounds of heaped stones. As a testimony to their age, most of the mounds have tall East African "pencil" cedar trees (*Juniperus procera*) or gnarled clumps of *Faurea* beechwood growing out of them; trees that must be a hundred, maybe even two hundred, years old.

The Sirikwa dwellings unearthed on the Cherangani are quite unlike anything ever built by the existing local tribes. Set in deep pits dug into the hillsides, they have each been found to comprise three or four distinct chambers, linked by tunnels and lined with intricately worked sandstone slabs. Roofed over with mud and dung, these pit dwellings—known as *tembes* or "Sirikwa holes"—were, it seems, extremely well concealed.

Excavation of one of the Kaisungurr mounds has led to suggestions that the Sirikwa may have cremated their dead. Charred traces of a funeral pyre were reportedly found on a broken sandstone construct underneath the monument of piled stones. Pot-shards dug up in the area have, rather fancifully, meanwhile, been likened in appearance to vessels unearthed in parts of Assyria.

Elgeyo-Marakwet cultivators on the steep Elgeyo Escarpment today make use of an ingenious network of irrigation conduits which they claim to be the legacy of the mysterious Sirikwa, whom they say perished in a terrible epidemic of plague that swept through the region in the early nineteenth century.

Another ancient pit-dwelling people, the Irakw or Mbulu, still persist on some of the remote hillsides in the northern "Crater Highlands" of Tanzania, in the vicinity of Mount Meru, as well as around both Ngorongoro Crater and Lake Manyara. Their *tembes* resemble the "Sirikwa holes" so closely that both are now thought to be the work of the same people. The similarity in the names, Irakw and Sirikwa, is thus thought to be more than just a coincidence.

Both groups have been speculatively linked to land-tilling descendants of east Africa's first invaders, the Neolithic "proto-Hamites" who are believed to have swept into the region from the north about 10,000 years ago. The Kadamas and the Tepes, isolated still on the remote heights of Kadam and Moroto, have likewise been linked to these early "proto-Hamitic" invaders, and not to the Bantu who came after (as the Rev Purvis and other early white travellers had supposed).

The Irakw and the Sirikwa, it is now supposed, were driven up onto the Cherangani as one people, by the Maasai and other Nilo-Hamitic invaders of the late Middle Ages. Here, it is speculated, they took to living underground in self-defence. In the eighteenth century, under still greater pressure from the Maasai and the Nandi tribes, many of them fled to the "Crater Highlands" of Tanzania, more than 400 km (approximately 250 miles) away.

The few Mbulu communities still living in Tanzania today have retained the strange, archaic tongue of their ancestors, many of whom, it would seem, perished here on the Cherangani, at the hands of the Maasai or by dint of some terrible, nameless plague. Beyond this highly speculative background, very little is known of the Sirikwa. Where, for instance, they picked up their advanced building techniques, almost certainly the first in the region to avail of hewn stone, remains a total mystery.

Looking at the varied artefacts they left scattered about on, and around, the Cherangani Hills, one cannot help but wonder: just who were these people?

The Ngurunit River in the eastern Ndotos following the seasonal rains.

For the nomadic herdsmen who roam this harsh land, drawing tepid water as they go from hand-dug wells along the river-beds, the forest-covered mountains are, and always have been, the only security against the ravages of these frequent and persistent droughts.

Year after year, in the seasonal dry spells between July and October and over January–February, when all the grazing on the plains has been utterly depleted, Samburu pastoralists are forced up onto the lofty green oases atop Kulal, Nyiru, the Ndotos, the Mathews Range (known locally as Ol Doinyo Lenkiyio) and Uaraguess, in the search for water and fresh pastures for their cattle.

On Mount Nyiru, the highest of the island mountains in Samburu territory, standing 2,753 m (9,032 ft) above sea level, the contrast between the cool summit oasis and the sweltering immensity of the desert below is at its most striking. A steep, three-hour climb from the Tuum Forest Station, at the western foot of the mountain near the dusty little village precinct of Tuum, is all that separates these astonishingly different worlds.

In the gentle dip of Nyiru's summit plateau, high above the desert haze and sheltered from the wind, stand dappled groves of magnificent old *Podocarpus* and East African "pencil" cedar trees, draped with long streamers of "old man's beard" lichen and enfolding lush, *Hypericum*-fringed glades crossed by tinkling mountain streams.

Late in March, with the first of the "long" rains, the *Podocarpus* trees, primitive conifers related to the yews, break into fruit, sporting myriads of fleshy, cherry-red receptacles with hard green berries "bonded" onto them, generally in pairs. The fleshy "centres", clear and white but having a sharp, resinous aftertaste, are like manna from heaven to the plateau's many resident Hartlaub's turacos which flutter about in the canopy overhead on brilliant scarlet wings.

At intervals the turacos all burst into song. Their loud, throaty utterances, excitedly repeated, reach brief crescendoes, first in one grove and then another, and so on all the way along the plateau until finally their message is carried out of earshot. Our Samburu guide, Kotel Lapadasa, said these birds, which he called "Nkarua" (an onomatopoeic name reminiscent of the Lukonjo "Sukurru" for the Ruwenzori turaco), were "telling the time, like they do every hour".

Around the open spots of greenery between the groves a host of starry yellow St John's wort flowers sparkle and dance in the sun, amid the steady buzzing of countless bees. A grass- and heather-covered ridge-line, rolling away to the north above the cedar cover, leads up to the rounded, summit boss of Mowo e Ngosowan: Samburu for "Horns of the Buffalo", the highest point on Nyiru.

On this ridge we found ourselves exposed, suddenly, to the full force of a lashing gale. "It never stops from blowing here," Kotel assured us. The prospect from the Buffalo Horns, the windswept northern tip of the mountain, is simply breathtaking. Snaking away over the north-north-western horizon, between jumbled walls of purple lava rubble, lies the shimmering silvery trough of Lake Turkana, the world's largest alkaline lake. Two hundred and fifty kilometres (approximately 150 miles) long and up to 45 km (approximately 25 miles) wide, this crocodile-infested lake was once part of the Nile's drainage, and, Nile crocodiles apart, still supports monstrous Nile perch, some weighing 100 kg (approximately 220 lbs) or more.

South-eastern slopes of Mount Nyiru from dry thornscrub on the south bank of the Muran Lugga near South Horr.

Mount Nyiru range from the west, near the village of Tuum.

It was at the foot of Nyiru's cedar-feathered cliffs of pinkish-brown granite ("nyiru" in Samburu means "brown") that Teleki and von Höhnel found the "slimy swamp" which earlier had saved them from almost certain death. A gruelling, three-day march across the virtual desert of the El Barta Plains had, by this time, pushed them to the limits of their endurance. Several members of their caravan had collapsed repeatedly on the journey; four had actually perished of exhaustion and thirst.

Parlera, the most prominent of Nyiru's west-facing cliffs, is said to owe its name, "Clear One" in Samburu, to its rôle as a natural beacon in guiding wandering herdsmen across the desert to the all-important, life-sustaining trickle of the Tuum River, alongside which the village-settlement of Tuum now lies. Maybe it was here, in the benign shadow of Parlera, that Teleki's party had been able to gather strength enough to undertake the final leg of the arduous journey to the lake.

The journey, a trek of well over 1,000 km (approximately 600 miles), had begun all of 13 months before, in Zanzibar. There, a General Lloyd Mathews, the then commander-in-chief of the army of the Sultan, had done much to help with the initial preparations. Just over a year into their safari, after marching over the Leroghi Plateau from Lake Baringo, Teleki and von Höhnel came upon the distant blue ramparts of Ol Doinyo Lenkiyio and the Ndoto Mountains and promptly, if rather vaguely, named this whole chain of mountains the Mathews Range.

What made Teleki's journey particularly arduous was that it was undertaken at the height of the devastating 1887–8 famine, itself brought on by years and years of unrelenting drought, the worst in tribal memory. The famine, however, was only the beginning of a whole chapter of hardships. It was followed in the 1890s by the grim period the Samburu refer to as the "mutai": literally, "the disasters".

First a smallpox epidemic broke out, killing many hundreds of their people. Then their herds too were decimated by successive epidemics of rinderpest and bovine pleuro-pneumonia. And then, on top of all this, came a series of Turkana invasions from the western deserts, where the epidemics had not struck. The Samburu, like other beaten tribes before them, were forced with the few cattle still remaining to them to take refuge on the mountains, living for the most part in the rockshelters, caves and forests on the upper slopes of Nyiru, the Ndotos, Ol Doinyo Lenkiyio and Kulal.

The livestock epidemics, though essentially cattle plagues, had a devastating effect on the area's wildlife: animals like buffalo and greater kudu (*Tragelaphus strepsiceros*), both seen in large numbers by Teleki, were particularly hard hit. The greater kudu, all but totally wiped out, has been very scarce here ever since. Today its range is confined to mountains like Kulal, Marsabit and the Ndotos.

On their remote mountain fastnesses the Samburu succeeded, gradually, in building up their herds. Many, of necessity, "turned dorobo" at this time, "eating fruits, hunting animals; rhinos, elephants, buffaloes, everything . . ." in order to survive. Most of the honey-hunting "dorobo" families active today on Kenya's northern mountains claim to be the descendants of those who "were forced to abandon pastoralism at the time of the *mutai*".

By all accounts, it was many years before the main body of the Samburu was ready, or able, to return to its customary pastoral way of life on the plains. The great spiritual significance the Samburu now attach to Mount Nyiru, in particular, seems to date from this period.

"For us, Nyiru is a sacred mountain," Andrew Dickson, the assistant chief of the Tuum Sub-Location, told us, "and all Samburu face towards it when they want to pray.

"And, when it comes to the time of the important ceremonies, like circumcision or *ilmugit* (the creation of the tribal age-sets), even the people from the other side of Samburu District have to wait," he said, "until a bull has been specially slaughtered at the top of Nyiru, in front of some chosen elders."

Certain cedar groves near Kusi Kussi, a large, flat-topped granite outcrop near the southern tip of Nyiru's sylvan island plateau, 10 km (approximately 6 miles) or so from the Buffalo Horns, are the sites favoured, Dickson indicated, for the carrying out of these ritual sacrifices. Kusi Kussi's sacred groves were aflame, when we passed through them, with brilliant red 'fireball' (*Scadoxus*) lilies.

"Kusi Kussi", like so many of the names for peaks and other features on both Nyiru and Kulal, is a Galla name, a carry-over from past Borana and Rendille occupations of the mountains. Eastern Cushitic peoples seem to have retained a foothold on Nyiru, or "Siil" as they called it, until well into the nineteenth century. One such people, the Wardai Galla, was reputedly overcome here by the Samburu in the 1840s, after mounting a long and desperate last stand on the mountain. They were never heard of again.

Kulal, 70 km (approximately 40 miles) north of Nyiru, was known as "Hanqu" by the Galla tribes. A savage-looking mountain, it straddles the infernal "badlands" of black lava rubble on the south-east shore of Lake Turkana, some of the most desolate terrain on earth. Though not particularly high by African standards, at just 2,293 m (approximately 7,523 ft) above sea level, it is a colossus in its desert world. The surrounding boulder-strewn flats, by comparison, are on average little more than 500 m (approximately 1,650 ft) in altitude.

The Horr Valley, the narrow gap between the cedar-clothed eastern walls of Nyiru and the gaunt crags of Ol Doinyo Mara (the "Speckled Mountain"), is

The fireball lily thrives in the dappled shade of Nyiru's cool cedar groves.

the gateway to the harsh volcanic world of Kulal and the Jade Sea. North of the gateway village of South Horr, set among tall, shady acacia trees on the banks of the Horr River, the rough, stony track that unwinds across the lava fields is barely fit even for four-wheel-drive vehicles.

Here, in a landscape that at first seems utterly devoid of all life, we saw several small herds of Grant's gazelles. And at one point we came upon a troupe of baboons, engaged in plucking live scorpions from under the lava boulders, disarming them of their stings with a deft twist of the wrist before swallowing them whole. Even here the desert is full of surprises.

Kulal itself is renowned, above all, for the fierce winds which seem to gust down incessantly from its slopes. The roving elephant hunter Arthur Neumann, who in 1896 became the first European to follow Teleki's footsteps around the lake, wrote of its being "difficult even to stand" in this continuous "avalanche" of wind[2].

Such howling "avalanches" are the result of a meteorological low pressure zone over Central Africa, which sucks prevailing south-westerly monsoon winds inland from the Indian Ocean, through the narrow gap dividing the Kenya/Tanzania highlands from those of Ethiopia. Kulal, positioned in the middle of this natural wind tunnel, is exposed to the full force of the blast.

The entire eastern side of Kulal's crater rim has collapsed, leaving a deep, scarred gorge known as El Kajarta, which almost splits the mountain in two. The only link, in fact, between the northern and southern summits of the massif, Arabal and Ladarabak, respectively, is a long, knife-edged spine of basalt, so steep that it was only traversed in 1983 by a party from Nairobi, led by Andrew Wielochowski.

Kulal, with its sharp, splayed ridges and rugged canyons, can look utterly forlorn. Yet on both its summits there are cool pockets of mist forest, moist enough for there to be orchids and mosses on many of the trees. These islands of forest are nurtured by highly localised rains, sometimes falls of up to 900 mm (35 inches) in a year. Just a few kilometres away, on the stark desert plains, the entire year's rainfall, by contrast, may amount to a mere 150 mm (six inches), or less.

East of Kulal lie the sun-baked wastes of the Chalbi and Koroli Deserts; the former an ancient dry lake bed of glaring white soda dust and peppery volcanic ash, flat and utterly desolate. Across this land of wind-spun dust and ghostlike heat mirages, some 100 km (approximately 60 miles) distant, stands the sprawling volcanic bulk of Marsabit Mountain, nearly 50 km (approximately 30 miles) broad and pocked with large explosion craters.

The mountain's string of dead volcanoes, though no more than 1,707 m (approximately 5,600 ft) above sea level, are the first substantial land-mass in the path of the monsoon winds from the east, and as such receive more rain than some mountains that are twice their height. Marsabit, in consequence, is graced with an extensive cover of dense mist forest, complete with dancing wild flowers, bright streams, cool wooded ravines and fern-fringed mossy glades. Its verdant slopes have, in addition, long been the domain of some of Africa's most celebrated big-tusked elephants, with ivory of 50 kg (approximately 110 lb) a side, or heavier.

Three of the great craters on Marsabit, when filled up by the rains, contain lakes of astonishing beauty and size. One, cradled in the highest of the dead volcanoes, is sometimes more than a kilometre across, a deep turquoise in colour and surrounded by luxuriant forest. The early wildlife photographer Martin Johnson and his wife Osa, who during the 1920s spent four years on Marsabit, gave the lake its present name: Lake Paradise.

---

[2] Neumann, A.: *Elephant Hunting in East Equatorial Africa*; Rowland Ward (London), 1898.

The lake was first seen by Europeans in 1895, when the American physician-turned-explorer Arthur Donaldson Smith and his companion, British taxidermist Edward Dodson, reached the top of Marsabit after an historic five-day march across the blistering deserts from Mount Kulal. This march was itself the culmination of a gruelling 15-month trek of more than 5,000 km (approximately 3,000 miles) from Berbera in the north-east, in what was then Somaliland. "Nothing," Donaldson Smith later wrote, "could be more charming than this Marsabit."[3]

South of Ol Doinyo Mara and the Horr Valley, near the notoriously treacherous Muran Lugga, a track branches off to the east, across the shimmering expanse of the Hedad and on over the kopje-studded Korante Plain to the wells and scattered dwellings of Ilaut, where Samburu cattle mingle with Rendille camels from the Kaisut Desert in the east. The view, south of the road, is dominated by the long north-eastern flank of the Ndoto Range of mountains.

Nearly 50 km (approximately 30 miles) in length, the Ndotos tend north-west to south-east, with the stark peak of Bokol, a bare rock dome 2,534 m (8,314 ft) above sea level, held up on sharp, angular ridges, as their north-western marker. Alimision, the highest of the Ndoto peaks at 2,637 m (8,651 ft) above sea level, is a huge, twisted pyramid of thinly grassed rock rising from the central portion of the range, high above the secluded mission settlement of Arsim.

In hurtling across the Korante Plain towards Ilaut, the eye is compulsively drawn to the looming bulk, ahead, of a massive, block-shaped sentinel of bare rock, gradually materialising out of the blue haze. This imposing form is Poi, unquestionably the real showpiece of Kenya's northern mountains.

Set just off the main body of the Ndoto Range, on a long, promontory-like

[3] Donaldson Smith, A.: *Through Unknown African Countries*; Edward Arnold (London), 1897.

The Ndoto Mountains from the eastern end.

easterly spur, Poi's towering-walls of ancient gneiss, sheer faces up to 700 m (approximately 2,300 ft) tall, soon dominate the landscape completely. Seen from the south-east, from the Ilaut-Ngurunit road which skirts its base, Poi looks just like an enormous, raised loaf of brown bread.

At 2,000 m (approximately 6,562 ft) above sea level, this gigantic loaf of rock stands more than a kilometre above the Kaisut Desert, stretching away towards Marsabit in the north-east. Its stupendous cliffs are pock-marked with large caves, many of them never visited by man. Some of these caves are doubtless used as nesting sites by the Rüppell's Griffon vultures (*Gyps rueppellii*) which spiral and soar endlessly in the thermals around the cliffs.

Poi's summit platform, a little kingdom in the sky, measuring roughly one kilometre (⅝ of a mile) by half a kilometre (⅓ of a mile), is patchily covered with woodland and grass. The only possible way up, for all but a few highly skilled, technical climbers, is via the main ridge-line in the west linking Poi with the central mass of the Ndotos.

The starting point for such an ascent is the col between Poi and Poi-kini ("little Poi"). The latter, shaped just like a perfect miniature of Poi when viewed from the north, is thought of as Poi's immortal new-born offspring, trotting along through time behind its giant mother, a mere fraction of the size.

For mountaineers, the vertical north, east and south faces of Poi hold some of the most testing big-wall climbing in East Africa. Only on one or two of the region's major high-altitude mountains, notably Mount Kenya, are there greater tests of a climber's skill and nerve. Yet because of its remoteness Poi has, as mountaineering challenges go, remained relatively little known, one of Africa's great climbing secrets.

Neither Poi's long south face nor its smaller north face has yet been conquered, and both are considered by some cragsmen to be impossible. For many years, as a consequence, climbing parties have concentrated their efforts on the narrow eastern face. The vertical wall here is one of Poi's tallest, rising sheer for some 650 m (approximately 2,000 ft). But its ledge systems, chimney-lines and cracks, all vital nooks and crannies that climbers look for when planning a new route, seemed to hold the best chances of success. However, of the many attempts that have so far been made on the face all but one has ended in failure.

The big breakthrough came in 1983, when two determined climbers, Andrew Wielochowski and Ron Corkhill, both now resident in the UK, finally succeeded, after three and a half days of hard, not to say nerve-wracking, technical rock work, in pioneering a route up Poi's spectacular east-facing buttress, directly above a sharp rock spike that has come to be known among climbers as The Shark's Tooth. Their feat has been described as "probably the most outstanding 'secret' achievement in recent Kenyan mountaineering history".

All but one of the 18 gruelling pitches on the climb, described in detail by Wielochowski in his *International Mountain Guide: East Africa* (West Col, 1986), were adjudged to be of Severe (Grade IV) standard, or higher; while at least three were accorded a Hard Very Severe (Grade VI) rating.

These gradings are reserved for high-risk vertical climbing of a kind which makes exacting demands on technical ability, since all the movements are strenuous and the hand- and foot-holds far from obvious. A Grade VI pitch is a section of a climb where these constraints are at their most pronounced, and where the exposure to serious risk is heightened accordingly. On Poi, there are points where the rock is friable, "rotten" in mountaineering parlance, and this, of course, poses an additional hazard.

East of Poi, marking the southern edge of the vast Kaisut Desert, are the

(*Opposite*) Poi, on a prominent easterly spur of the Ndoto Mountains, offers some of the most testing technical climbing in East Africa.

(*Following pages*) Evening light catches the isolated peaks of Baio, near south edge of the Kaisut Desert.

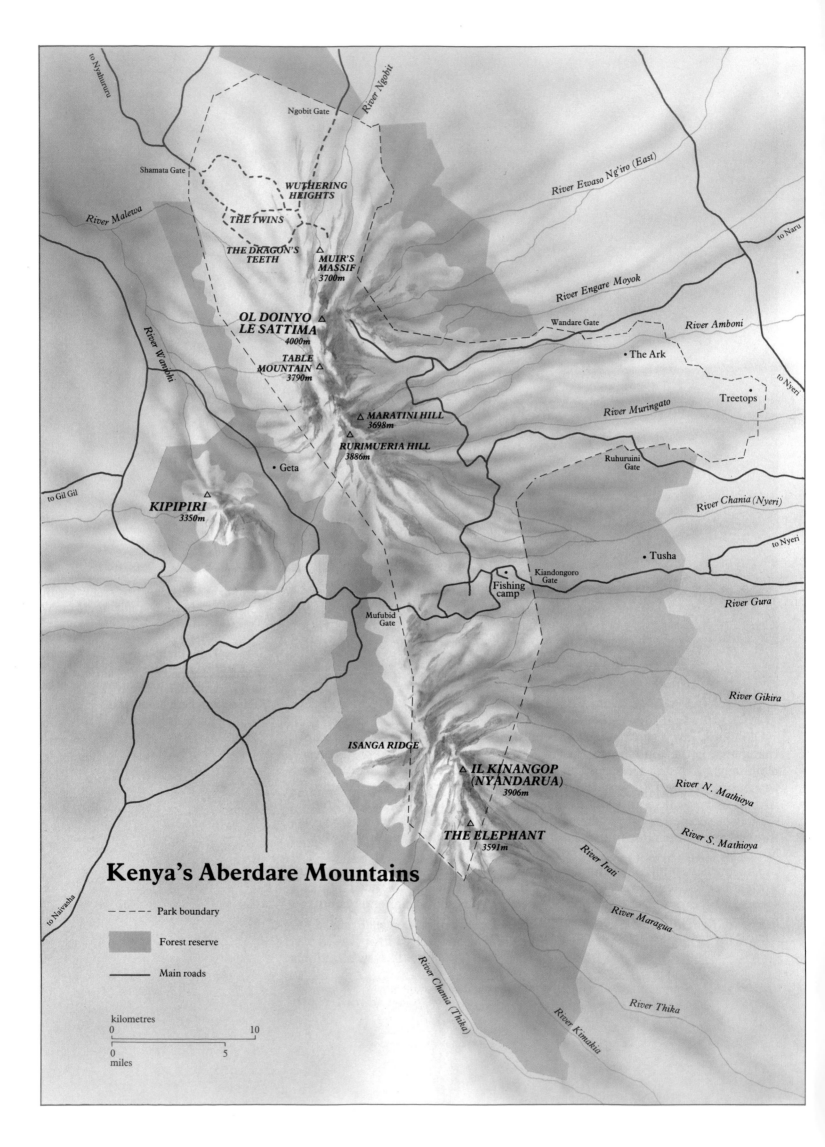

Ngobit Gate

to Nyahururu

River Ngobit

River Malewa

Shamata Gate

WUTHERING HEIGHTS

THE TWINS

THE DRAGON'S TEETH

△ MUIR'S MASSIF 3700m

OL DOINYO LE SATTIMA △ 4000m

TABLE MOUNTAIN △ 3790m

River Wanjohi

△ MARATINI HILL 3698m

△ RURIMUERIA HILL 3886m

• Geta

KIPIPIRI △ 3350m

to Gil Gil

River Ewaso Ng'iro (East)

River Engare Moyok

Wandare Gate

River Amboni

to Naru

• The Ark

Treetops •

to Nyeri

River Muringato

Ruhuruini Gate

River Chania (Nyeri)

• Tusha

to Nyeri

Mufubid Gate

Fishing camp

Kiandongoro Gate

River Gura

River Gikira

ISANGA RIDGE

△ **IL KINANGOP (NYANDARUA)** 3906m

△ **THE ELEPHANT** 3591m

River N. Mathioya

River S. Mathioya

River Irati

River Maragua

River Chania (Thika)

River Kimakia

River Thika

Kenya's Aberdare Mountains

- - - Park boundary

Forest reserve

—— Main roads

to Naivasha

kilometres
0   10

0   5
miles

6 · Hides and Sleeping Places: Kenya's Aberdare Mountains

Gordon Boy

Bomb scars, grim reminders of Britain's efforts to quell the Mau Mau uprising of the 1950s, are still discernible on the rugged slopes of the Aberdare Mountains, scene of the most savage fighting of Kenya's troubled Emergency years. The range, last major stronghold of the Mau Mau revolt, lies just a few hours' drive north of Nairobi, where it forms a lengthy rampart of high ground between Mount Kenya in the east and the lake-studded void of the Eastern, or Gregory, Rift Valley in the west.

For nearly 60 km (approximately 40 miles) the Aberdares, tending north-south, maintain an elevation of 3,000 m (9,850 ft) or more, above sea level. The two highest peaks—Ol Doinyo Le Sattima in the north, at 4,000 m (13,123 ft), and Il Kinangop (Nyandarua), 3,906 m (12,816 ft) up—stand 34 km (approximately 20 miles) apart, near opposite ends of this long, rolling strip of open moorland terrain.

The moorland hills, weather-beaten into soft, graceful curves, reveal little of the range's fiery, volcanic past. This past saw the mountains take shape as an immense central volcano, active between roughly 6.5 and 5 million years ago, long before the adjacent section of the Rift, dominated by Lake Naivasha and Mount Longonot, assumed its present form.

Today the range is perhaps less than half its former size, having been split, about 2 million years ago, by an event geologists have called the Sattima Fault. This, coupled with further such bouts of violent down-faulting along the east Rift margin, resulted in the collapse of the entire western side of the volcano.

The western slopes are consequently precariously steep. Their once far gentler aspects lie buried underneath the broad Kinangop Plateau, the flattish lava "step" between the mountain wall and the Rift floor. A bleak and windy place, this plateau, averaging an altitude of some 2,560 m (8,400 ft), was turned into a battlefield with the outbreak of the nineteenth-century Maasai civil wars.

Jutting out onto the plateau, on a high westerly spur of the mountains, sits the bold, outlying peak of Kipipiri, 3,350 m (10,990 ft) above sea level. A squat basalt dome, Kipipiri effectively divides the Kinangop Plateau from the more northerly Wanjohi Valley, home during the 1930s of the infamous "Happy Valley" community of sybaritic British aristocrats.

The weather-rounded bulk of Ol Doinyo Le Sattima, the "Mountain of the Young Bull" of the Maasai, stands well back from the deep Rift chasm, some 14 km (approximately 9 miles) north-east of Kipipiri. Flanked by other knuckle-shaped hummocks and bare, knob-like rocks of only slightly lower elevation, Sattima, from most angles, does not stand out as the obvious high-point of the Aberdares.

North of Sattima, towards the billowy expanses of Wuthering Heights, on the far northern moors, there persist odd relics of the forgotten volcanic past of

Cascade on the Aberdare moorlands, birthplace of many of Kenya's major rivers.

"Out! Out!", the alarm reputedly raised by lookouts at the secret oathing ceremonies to warn participants of a police approach.

Support from Mau Mau sympathisers in the Kikuyu reserves on the eastern Aberdare foothills meant the fugitive gangs were assured, at first, of a ready supply of food, weaponry and other provisions. Their forest hideouts, or *ihingo*, meanwhile, were so expertly concealed that, as one British officer conceded, it "was possible to pass within a few yards of one without having any idea of its existence".

From their mountain hideouts the guerrilla gangs, armed mainly with *simis* (double-edged slashing swords) and *pangas* (machetes) but carrying an assortment of pistols, captured rifles and ingenious, if unreliable, home-made guns, pulled off a string of bold, sometimes crushingly effective, raids on the guard-posts and forts stationed around the Aberdares by the British and colonial forces. Local Kikuyu smallholders, branded "passive terrorists" by the British and "spineless loyalists" by the Mau Mau, were among the conflict's worst-hit victims, suffering atrocities from both sides.

On the mountains the government forces, for all their far greater firepower, could make little headway against the activists. Again and again, superior Mau Mau bushcraft made a mockery of forest operations mounted by the British Army units and KAR (King's African Rifles) battalions. The white-settler force, the Kenya Regiment, fared only marginally better.

Years afterwards, Mau Mau bush skills would be put to brilliant effect in combating poaching in both the Aberdare and Mount Kenya National Parks. In 1959 Bill Woodley, then warden of Mountain National Parks and himself a veteran of service with the Kenya Regiment, took the bold and, at the time, highly controversial step of employing ex-Mau Mau activists as armed forest rangers.

The step, for which Woodley was widely blackballed by the European community of the day, turned out to be an unqualified success: "It is an accepted fact," he could state in 1977, towards the end of his mammoth stint in getting the two parks off the ground, "that there is far less poaching in the forests of the Aberdares and Mount Kenya than in any other national park.

"The reason for this," he explained, "was put to me by a Kikuyu ex-poacher: 'It is too much of a risk, Bwana. Your rangers were Mau Mau. They can see better, hear better, and move faster than any of us.'"[1]

During the early years of the Emergency, Mau Mau bushcraft had done nothing but frustrate the British. And it was as a measure of this frustration that Royal Air Force (RAF) Lincoln, Meteor and Harvard aircraft, pinpointing what they took to be the Mau Mau hideouts, resorted to bombing the high Aberdare forests. However, these raids had little or no effect on the rebels, serving only to bolster the prestige of one of the Mau Mau witchdoctors, Kingori, who had once prophesied that "rocks of fire would fall out of the sky".

Wild animals, instead, were the main casualties of the RAF raids. Rhinos, elephants, buffaloes and antelopes were among those slaughtered, maimed or otherwise wounded by the explosions. For years afterwards the range's Colobus and Sykes' monkeys would shin down the forest trees for cover on first hearing the steady drone of an approaching aeroplane.

Filled up by the rain, the bomb craters became waterholes at which game would congregate in the evenings. Today, the Aberdare bomb scars, stamped and wallowed in by countless animals, are mere weathered depressions, wounds that have healed virtually beyond recognition.

Back in 1954, two years into the Emergency, the Aberdare Mountains were under siege. The rebel gangs, cut off from their supply networks, were forced to live by trapping and *shamba*-raiding. Their dwindling stocks of ammunition they reserved for the enemy, now closing in from all sides and driving them higher and higher up the mountain slopes. The colonial forces, resigned to Mau Mau superiority in "bush combat", had by this time resorted to "pseudo-gang" tactics. Mau Mau detainees, turned collaborator, were issued with revolvers and persuaded to infiltrate and capture the gangs of their former colleagues.

Foremost of these gangs was that led by the charismatic Dedan Kimathi, most powerful and feared of all the Mau Mau leaders. By the end of 1955, when only a hard-core of some 1,500 guerrillas remained on the Aberdares, "pseudo-gang" activity had come to be dominated by what the colonials would call "the hunt for Kimathi", their most wanted man.

The "hunt" centred on two of the most intractable and densely wooded parts of the Aberdares: the jumbled ridges and deep valleys of Ruthaithi, now the Aberdares Salient, site of Kenya's two best known forest lodges, Treetops and The Ark; and the vast, neighbouring expanse of higher ground known as "the

[1](quoted in) Holman, D.: *Elephants at Sundown: The Story of Bill Woodley*; W. H. Allen (London), 1978.

(*Following pages*) Stormclouds gather over the slopes of lofty Ol Doinyo Le Sattima, the highpoint of the Aberdares.

Bamboo forest characteristic of the Aberdares.

Morning mist on the Aberdares.

Mwathe", after the legendary hunter credited with having roamed these great mountains in ancient times.

The fire which gutted the original Treetops in 1954 was one of the more trifling deeds ascribed to Kimathi's gang. A mere guest-hut-cum-viewing-platform nestled in the high boughs of a giant *mugumo* (wild fig) tree, Treetops had gained international renown as the place where, two years earlier, Britain's Princess Elizabeth was staying on the night she became Queen on the death of her father King George VI.

The *mugumo* and *mururua* (Cape chestnut) trees, whose natural hollows and fissures Kimathi used as "letterboxes" for trading messages with other gangs, still flourish in the Salient, dumb to all the bloody skirmishes that flared up around them in 1956, in the hit-and-run battle that developed between Kimathi's henchmen and their "pseudo Mau Mau" pursuers. Rhinos, sent crashing blindly through the undergrowth, posed an additional hazard for the combatants. The wounded, like the dead, were left, more often than not, to be fought over by scavenging hyaenas.

Through all this Kimathi, arch malcontent, seemed to bear a charmed life. Uncanny premonitions, vouchsafed to him in dreams, enabled him to carry off a series of narrow, seemingly miraculous, escapes. This "sixth sense" of his seemed, to his diminishing band of followers, to bear out his repeated claims to god-given powers.

During the last months of Kimathi's reign on the Aberdares, the depleted band sat huddled in the mist under skimpy bivouacs of buckskin, draped tent-like over bamboo-culm supports. For warmth they wore dirty buckskin coats, or *githii*, stitched together with forest twines or fine leather strips. Their hair, smeared in animal fat, stood up in long, plaited spikes, or hung down, shoulder-length, in matted "dreadlocks". There is a Kikuyu folktale that relates how the Aberdare Mountains, long ago, became a place of perpetual cold and soaking grey mists when an elderly hunter, Mutanga Riya, took off his *githii* one day and inadvertently hung it over the sun.

Kimathi was captured on October 21, 1956, four years to the day after the proclamation of the Emergency. Alone and half-starved following the capture of his woman, Wanjiru, and the rest of his gang, he was apprehended in a police ambush, after being shot in the leg while on a desperate foray into the Kikuyu *shambas* at the lower edge of the Salient forest. In a curious twist, his favourite *mugumo* "prayer-tree" on the Aberdares (the *mugumo* fig is traditionally sacred to all Kikuyu) came crashing down within hours of his capture.

Early in 1957, after standing trial in his native Nyeri, Kimathi was hanged. Today he is remembered as one of Kenya's leading freedom-fighters, and has been accorded the status of a national hero; one of Nairobi's main streets is named after him. By the time of Kimathi's defeat the Mau Mau rebellion, sapped from within by quarrels between rival factions, had all but lost direction. The forest fighting, which left more than 13,000 dead, had been superseded by the political developments that in 1963 would culminate in Kenya's *uhuru*. Those rebel groups that remained, high up on the Aberdares, hunched around covert fires in their scraps of reeking hide, had played their part.

Such, once, had been the plight of small, remnant bands of an aboriginal hunting people, the Gumba; driven up onto these same cold mountain fastnesses more than 150 years before, during the last few decades of the eighteenth century. The Gumba, though, later vanished altogether. They were a pit-dwelling, pygmoid people, one of two hunter-gatherer communities whom the immigrant "Eastern" Bantu ancestors of the Kikuyu, sweeping in from the north-east in the late seventeenth century, encountered in the dense forests around Mount Kenya and the Aberdares. The newcomers, struck by their diminutive stature and menacing bushcraft, called them the "Maitha a Ciana", literally, "the child-sized enemy".

Advanced iron-working skills acquired from the Gumba provided the Kikuyu pioneers with efficient tools for clearing the ground before them for settlement and cultivation, on their westerly advance towards the Aberdares. The pygmoid bowmen, unable to check this agricultural onslaught, fast depriving them of their ancestral hunting-grounds, retreated, as the Mau Mau would do after them, into the high forests on the mountains.

Here they mingled with a second forest-dwelling aboriginal community, that of the bushmanoid Okiek hunter-gatherers, whom the Maasai, when they encountered them, called the Dorobo. The Okiek, referred to simply as the "Athi" ("huntsmen") by the advancing Kikuyu, were likewise soon displaced from their ancestral lands.

The retreating bands of Okiek and Gumba bowmen were joined in resisting Kikuyu expansion by another tribe, thought to have been the pastoralist Barabaig (or Barabiu), the region's earliest Hamitic invaders. Not a forest people, the latter were brought into conflict with the Kikuyu only through being driven up onto the highlands by the Maasai.

The Barabaig, in particular, proved to be formidable foes, and were not overcome until well into the 1800s, when they were routed by the combined might of the Kikuyu and the Purko (or Burugo) clan of the Maasai. Kikuyu–Maasai relations, cemented by this alliance, deteriorated with the outbreak of the Maasai civil wars of the 1860s and 1870s.

These wars, fought on the great plateaux around the Aberdares, involved a long-running series of pitched battles between the Purko and their one-time allies the Laikipiak, a leading faction of the Kwavi, the so-called "semi-pastoral" Maasai. The Purko it was who eventually prevailed. The depleted

Hushed forests of "pencil" cedar grace the northern Aberdare steeps, below the storm-drenched tussock moors.

Laikipiak, driven off in all directions, were later further decimated by the natural disasters of the 1880s: drought; famine; smallpox; cattle plagues, and crop-invading locust swarms.

The Purko, meanwhile, named the great, knob-crested southern peak of the Aberdares "Ilkinaapop"—"rulers of the land"—to commemorate their famous, if ultimately pyrrhic, victory. The name, later spelt "Il Kinangop" by British land-surveyors and cartographers, still stands today.

To the Kikuyu settlers, exposed suddenly to the depredations of both the warring Maasai and the Arab and Swahili slave-raiders and trading caravans, now venturing inland in increasing numbers with their muzzle-loading "sticks of fire", the peak was, first and foremost, a place of refuge. Easily the most striking feature on the Aberdare skyline, it became known as "Kea-

Nyandarua"—"mountain of hides or sleeping places". Nyandarua, now as then, is also the Kikuyu name for the range as a whole.

The scene which greeted the approach of the range's first European visitor was one of nauseating carnage. British explorer Joseph Thomson, rounding the northern slopes in 1883 while on his historic trek through Maasailand, found the route—a Maasai stock trail—to be "dotted with the dried carcasses of hundreds of diseased cattle", victims of the devastating rinderpest and bovine pleuro-pneumonia epidemics then rife in the land. Thomson it was who, finding the Maasai to have no general name for these mountains, dubbed them the Aberdare Range after his patron Lord Aberdare, then president of London's Royal Geographical Society.

For Thomson, as for other Europeans after him, the rolling Aberdare landscapes, "studies in beautiful nature-curves and variegated greens", complete with cold, bracing winds, driving "Scotch" mists and nightly frosts, hardly seemed a part of Africa at all. Such vistas, "rousing stirring memories of home scenes", had Thomson, to the great astonishment of his shivering entourage, "dancing about outside (the tents) with patriotic glee".

Hard on Thomson's heels came other Europeans, among them missionaries, adventurers and empire-builders. The Imperial British East Africa (IBEA) Company, granted a royal charter in 1888, built forts and trading depots around the Aberdares, effectively paving the way for British rule. By 1895 the colonisation of Kenya, as part of the British East Africa Protectorate, was a *fait accompli*.

The farming potential of the Aberdare highlands was passed over, initially, by company agents and early British administrators, obsessed only with the promised wealth of inaccessible Uganda. The Uganda railroad, construction of which began in earnest in 1895, would be the cherished link with the riches of the African interior. By 1899 this "highway to Uganda" had got as far as

Southern Aberdare moorland, from the Kiandongoro Fishing Camp.

Nairobi, then no more than a large rail depot known as Mile 326.

By way of justifying the enormous cost of the railroad, the British government instituted special land schemes to encourage British settlement. Out of this came the administration's dream of a "White Highlands", with the Aberdare Mountains at its centre. White settlers, streaming into the region in the early 1900s, soon turned this dream into reality.

For this purpose, land was taken from both the Kikuyu and the Maasai, for whom separate "reserves" were hastily set aside. This, coupled with the atrocities perpetrated in the name of spreading British rule by the swash-buckling antics of some of the military commanders, kindled the resentment that, half a century afterwards, fanned by the winds of incipient pan-African nationalism, would flare up as the Mau Mau revolt.

Turn-of-the-century Kikuyu resistance, confined to isolated warrior groups holed up in the lower Aberdare forests, was easily contained by the British. Opposition, where it did arise, was met with crushing, punitive raids, launched from the military outposts around the mountains. Many a punitive expedition into the Aberdare forests was carried out under Captain (later Colonel) Richard Meinertzhagen, of the Third KAR Battalion, who was stationed at Fort Hall (now Murang'a) and at Nyeri between 1902 and 1904. In his *Kenya Diary, 1902–1906* Meinertzhagen records the gory details of one of his "most un-pleasant duties": "The natives caught a settler yesterday, a white man who was trying to buy sheep from the Kihimbuini people," reads his entry for September 7, 1902. "They dragged him to a village near the forest, where they pegged him down . . . and wedged his mouth open; then the whole village, man, woman and child, urinated in his mouth till he was drowned.

"I have never conceived that such a horrible death could have been in-vented," he wrote, ". . . [and] Maycock has given me a free hand to deal with this village, which I shall do at dawn tomorrow . . ."

The reprisal, described in his entry for the next day, was simply devastating: "Every soul was either shot or bayoneted . . . We burned all the huts and razed the banana plantations to the ground . . . The whole affair took so short a time that the sun was barely up before we beat a retreat to our main camp."

Meinertzhagen was also a naturalist of some repute and, earlier in 1902, in the course of a land survey mission on the Aberdares, had become the first European to make an ascent of Kinangop peak. He wrote:

We climbed up and up, the temperature fell lower and lower and our breath came quicker and quicker as we got into the alpine zone of tropical Africa. After 5 hours' stiff climb (from our camp near the headwaters of the Meragua River) we reached the summit of the main ridge, and there was Kinangop peak about half a mile to the north.

I made a rapid rush to get to the top, and succeeded after an hour's scramble over wet rocks in getting a magnificent view of the whole Kikuyu country in the east, with Mount Kenya in the distance, while to the west lay the deep Rift Valley with the huge lake of Naivasha gleaming in the sun. To the south lay expanses of forest with the vast Athi Plains stretching towards Kilimanjaro, which was just visible . . .

The country on top was open but very rough. Huge boulders lay about in confusion, clothed in moss and fern; stunted bushes grew between the boulders, often festooned with fantastic lichen. On the summit of Kinangop I built a cairn about 6 feet high, and in it I placed a bottle of beer with a request that should it be unearthed by anyone at some future date he should drink my health and drop me a line to 25 Rutland Gate.[2]

---

[2] Meinertzhagen, R.: *Kenya Diary 1902–1906*; Eland Books (London), paperback reissue, 1983.

Passing through Tusha, a small settlement at the eastern foot of the range, on his way up, Meinertzhagen came upon three Italian White Fathers. Their chief interest, he observed, seemed to be in "enticing young boys and girls into their mission, and under the pretence of teaching religion . . . introducing them to a code of immorality completely foreign to the Wakikuyu".

"They are certainly not 'white', but doubtless will soon be fathers," was his caustic comment.

Five years later in 1907 Chauncey Hugh Stigand, a British Army captain on leave from the Equatorial campaign in the Sudan, "found it necessary to climb the high peak of Kinangop while sketching for the East Africa survey" during a hunting expedition to the mountains. His ascent, via the upper Tulasha Valley, after a long, southward traverse from the head of the Wanjohi Valley and over the "high pass" between outlying Kipipiri and the Aberdares proper, was the first by a European from the western, or Naivasha/Rift Valley, side of the range. Stigand later wrote:

> The last two thousand feet were bare, that is to say, there were patches of bare rock, coarse grass in isolated tufts, a giant sort of groundsel, and a few other mountain plants, but no thick or high vegetation . . . Elephant tracks led up to within a few hundred feet of the top, whilst a rhino track reached practically the summit . . .
>
> From a distance the mountain seemed to have a cairn perched on its summit. This in reality was a great block of rock about the size of a house . . . surmounted by a black iron arrangement shaped like a large stable lantern, on the top of a pole and guyed down to the rock with four bars of iron.[3]

Eroded lava on the Aberdares sometimes takes extraordinary shapes.

On one side of the lantern-shaped iron box Stigand found a small door, with a catch. This he promptly opened. "I do not think I have ever felt such a shock of surprise in my life," he wrote. "If ten rattlesnakes had come rushing out, I should have been prepared to meet them. But what I actually saw was a small shrine and a picture of the Virgin Mary."

One of the renegade "White Fathers" of Tusha, Father Fillipe Perlo, had, it transpired, led a mission delegation up onto the summit of Kinangop earlier that year. On erecting the shrine the whole party had, as it turned out, celebrated "high mass".

On his way down the mountain in 1902, Meinertzhagen caught his first glimpse of the giant forest hog, the "enormous black pig" that was later named *Hylochoerus meinertzhageni meinertzhageni* in his honour. Though certain from the moment he saw it that the pig was "new to science", it was another two years before he was successful in shooting a specimen, thus enabling him to dispatch a skull, along with a complete skin, to the British Museum in London for verification.

Giant forest hog.

The tough skin of the giant pig had long been prized by the Kikuyu and the Maasai, who called its owner *numira* and *elguia* respectively, for its excellent qualities as a shield-making material. As such, the skins were a much sought-after object of Kikuyu/Maasai barter with the Dorobo huntsmen of the forests. The giant forest hog was the last of Africa's large mammals to reveal itself to western science.

On the same downhill trek from the Kinangop, Meinertzhagen glimpsed another creature he had never seen before, "a huge red antelope of sorts with white stripes". Only later in 1902 was this, the shy eastern race of the bongo (*Boocercus eurycerus isaaci*), identified by science as a subspecies distinct from its more widespread western counterpart, *Boocercus eurycerus eurycerus*, which

---

[3] Stigand, C. H.: *Hunting the Elephant in Africa*; Macmillan (New York), 1913.

Moorland, seen through a gap in the Dragon's Teeth, a scatter of strange lava boulders near the northern tip of the lengthy Aberdare range.

frequents the great rainforests of Zaïre, Gabon and other west and central African countries. Today the eastern bongo is found in groups of any size or number only on the Aberdares.

Reports of other unrecorded animals greatly boosted scientific interest in the fauna of the Aberdares. Naturalists, eager to make startling discoveries, were drawn to the range's moors and forests. Of the quests that followed, none was so determined as that undertaken in the 1920s by British naturalist Kenneth Gandar Dower, whose search for the legendary "spotted lion" of the Aberdare Moorlands extended to several lengthy expeditions.

Gandar Dower's search, though spurred early on by the acquisition of some "spotted" lion pelts which had found their way down into Kikuyu hands from Dorobo hunters on the mountains, went unrewarded. One of the "mystery" pelts—now thought to be that of an immature lion—belongs to London's Natural History Museum.

The enigma of the "spotted lion" was to linger on for many years afterwards, fostered in part by the fact that the lions that *were* sometimes encountered on the rolling moors had, in the cold, developed longer, darker coats. Indeed, until as recently as 1960, these lions were still widely thought of as belonging to a distinct montane subspecies.

It is possible, moreover, that the golden cat (*Felis aurata*), the most seldom seen of African felines, may have helped to propagate the legend. For it was only in the late 1960s, when some golden cat furs—small but tawny in colour, with dark spots on the flank areas—turned up in a poachers' hideout deep in the "black forest", that the presence on the Aberdares of this elusive predator was finally established. Previously, its range in Kenya had been thought to be confined to the Mau Range and Mount Elgon, west of the Rift Valley.

One phenomenon that has never been in any doubt is the extraordinarily high incidence, among certain of the Aberdare predators, of melanism: the sporting of an all-black coat. Jet-black servals (*Felis serval*), in particular, can often be seen slinking about over the open moors below the peaks, where they subsist largely on rodents and francolins. Even the sight of a melanistic leopard, black panther supreme, exploding from a thicket of pathside heather, is not considered to be all that unusual here.

In the late-1920s the Aberdares, ever a naturalist's paradise, came to be associated with wild life of an altogether different order. For it was at this time that the small but notorious "Happy Valley" community of aristocratic lotus-eaters settled in the broad Wanjohi Valley, nestled between the bold hump of Kipipiri and the great, frowning wall of the range's north-westerly escarpment.

Here it was that Josslyn Hay, later the 22nd Earl of Erroll, and his twice-divorced mistress Lady Idina Gordon set up home in 1925, having eloped together the year before from England. Their mansion, "Clouds", soon became the hub of a wanton feudal paradise that was to endure for almost 20 years, until well into World War Two. Devoted only to the pursuit of pleasure, "Happy Valley" residents were oblivious to the hardships then preoccupying fellow European settlers who, in striving to transform neighbouring tracts of the "White Highlands" from bush into farmland, were confronted with all manner of obstacles: strange soils; an unfamiliar climate; infestations of tropical insect pests, and a whole catalogue of unknown crop- and stock-diseases.

Life in Happy Valley, by contrast, revolved around an endless spree of "house parties", renowned above all for the reckless drinking, drug-taking, wild orgies and wife-swapping they entailed. Even the Wanjohi River, tumbling down off the forested saddle between Kipipiri and Sattima, was said to run, not with water, but with cocktails and champagne.

The party ended amid the scandal that erupted following Erroll's murder in January 1941. Shot in the head, his body was found slumped in the footwell of his Buick in a ditch by the side of the road on the outskirts of Nairobi. The murder was never solved, and has been a subject of keen speculation ever since, resurrected most recently in James Fox's book *White Mischief* (1982), and in the Michael White/Michael Radford film of the same name, released in 1988.

Only in the wake of Erroll's murder did a full picture emerge of the extravagant excesses of life in the Happy Valley of the 1930s. Many Valley residents were to claim, in true Romantic fashion, that they had been smitten by the exhilarating grandeur of the Aberdare landscapes. And, letting the deliciously bracing mountain air go to their heads, they had succumbed to what became known as the "three As": altitude, alcohol . . . and adultery.

The head waters of the Tana River.

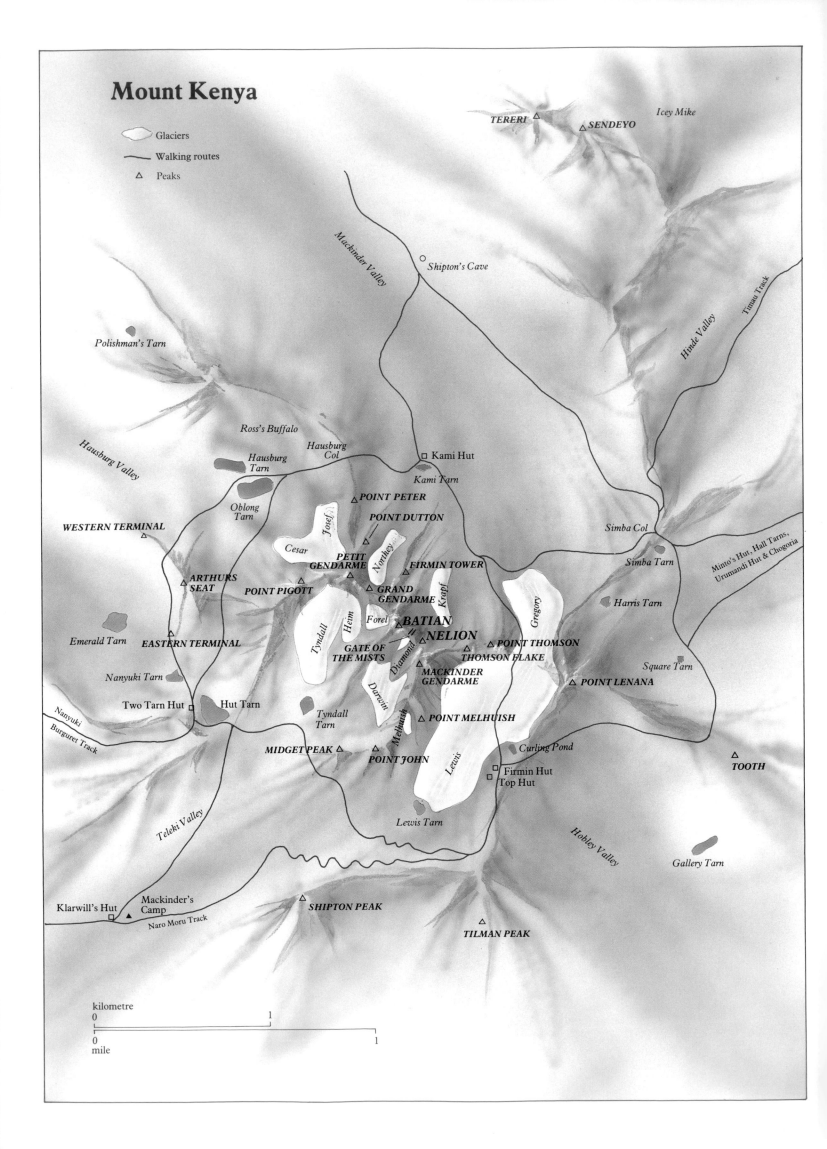

Mount Kenya

Glaciers

Walking routes

△ Peaks

TERERI △   △ *SENDEYO*   *Icey Mike*

Mackinder Valley   ○ *Shipton's Cave*

Hinde Valley   *Timau Track*

Polishman's Tarn

Ross's Buffalo

Hausburg Valley   *Hausburg Col*   □ *Kami Hut*

Hausburg Tarn   *Kami Tarn*

Oblong Tarn   △ *POINT PETER*

WESTERN TERMINAL △   *Josef*   *POINT DUTTON*

Simba Col

Cesar   *PETIT GENDARME*   *Northey*   *FIRMIN TOWER*

Minto's Hut, Hall Tarns, Urumandi Hut & Chogoria

Simba Tarn

ARTHURS SEAT △   **POINT PIGOTT** △   △ **GRAND GENDARME**   *Krapf*

Harris Tarn

Emerald Tarn   *Heim*   *Forel*   **BATIAN**   *Gregory*

EASTERN TERMINAL △   *Tyndall*   **"NELION**   △ **POINT THOMSON**

Nanyuki Tarn   **GATE OF THE MISTS**   *Diamond*   **THOMSON FLAKE**

Square Tarn

Two Tarn Hut □   *Hut Tarn*   *Darwin*   **MACKINDER GENDARME**

△ **POINT LENANA**

Nanyuki   *Tyndall Tarn*   *Melhuish*   △ **POINT MELHUISH**

Burguret Track   *Curling Pond*

MIDGET PEAK △   △   *Lewis*   □ *Firmin Hut* *Top Hut*

△ **TOOTH**

POINT JOHN

Teleki Valley   *Lewis Tarn*   *Hobley Valley*

Gallery Tarn

Klarwill's Hut □   *Mackinder's Camp* ▲   △ **SHIPTON PEAK**

Naro Moru Track

△ **TILMAN PEAK**

kilometre

0   1

0   1

mile

7 · Monarch of Mountains: Mount Kenya

Iain Allan

Kenya is a country of intricate contrasts. From its palm-fringed, white shores on the Indian Ocean, it unfolds inland for several hundred kilometres like a great parched carpet—a desolate, dry land of gnarled, thorny scrub. The transition from semi-desert to rolling plains is a gentle one sloping to 1,250 and 1,520 m (4,100 and 5,000 ft), and from these plains, if the day is clear, one can see the western horizon rising higher in ever darkening shades of green, as it lifts to the densely forested edges of the Great Rift Valley. This is an area of immense, unexpected geological confusion—a land in turmoil, as if taken by surprise when the Rift formed, and now unable to work out which shape to be. The sides of deep, green river-valleys rise to become hills, with expectations of stature and greatness, but then somehow manage to fall just short of nobility. But further north, up the eastern edge of the Rift, the land comes to terms with itself. The hills become more clearly defined and, with the Aberdare Mountains, more distinguished. The Aberdares however are merely a beginning, for somehow the entire country is coming together. Hill and ridge connect hill and ridge until finally they culminate in a magnificent mountain soaring 5,180 m (17,000 ft) into the sky, its icy summit tooth daring even the Equator, which traverses its northern slopes, to defy it. No country could have a finer symbol.

Mount Kenya is 5,199 m (17,058 ft) high, and a little over 100 km (approximately 60 miles) in diameter. It is an extinct, ancient volcano whose period of activity was 3.1 to 2.6 million years ago, when it probably rose to over 7,600 m (25,000 ft) with a shape resembling that of Kilimanjaro. Today the shape of Mount Kenya belies the fact that it was ever a volcano at all. There is little trace of a crater left, so beaten has the mountain become through time and countless eruptions; but its majestically battered peaks, draped by 11 glaciers, radiate an air of supreme elegance. From the plains, the peaks of Mount Kenya seem to float like a distant fortress in the sky, or perhaps as the Wakamba people, who dwell some 200 km (approximately 125 miles) away, used to say, like a "Cock Ostrich", when its white glaciers contrast with the dark rock, appearing like the black and white plumage of the male ostrich. This could well be the origin of the word "Kenya", for in the Wakamba language "Kiinya" means "The Hill of the Cock Ostrich".

The heart of Mount Kenya lies in the thick, semi-tropical rain forests which grace its lower slopes up to an altitude of 3,350 m (11,000 ft). These forests begin between 2,130 and 2,450 m (7,000 and 8,000 ft) from the uppermost point reached by the fertile farms or *shambas* of the Kikuyu people. Giant trees of camphor wood, "pencil" cedar, *Podocarpus* and East African olive, draped by vine-like lianes, rise above a tangled profusion of dripping ferns, nettles and bamboo. It is a difficult area for man to penetrate, and because of this it is home to herds of Cape buffalo and elephant, as well as bushbuck and the occasional

Malachite sunbird.

Groundsel on Mount Kenya.

Lobelia leaf cluster on Mount Kenya.

Black rhino (*Diceros bicornis*). Colobus monkeys frequent the trees and the forest is roamed by predators like spotted hyaena (*Crocuta crocuta*) and leopard. Every afternoon this dank, lost world emits a temptation which the very air cannot resist, and a grey blanket of cloud slowly but thoroughly wraps its mysterious arms around the forest's endless canopy.

With dramatic suddenness the forests end at 3,350 m (11,000 ft) with the precision brought about by a master landscape gardener, and the moorlands begin. This region which extends upwards to 4,300 m (14,100 ft) offers more of a compromise and compares with the stark beauty of the Scottish Highlands. Tussock grasses, with intermittent heather growing occasionally over 3 m (10 ft) in height, gradually transform into the drier world of the outlandish, tree-like giant groundsels (*Senecio keniodendron*) and lobelia. The area is studded with rock islands of porous, volcanic ashes and agglomerates, standing out like dark, incongruous sentinels. Big game is rarely seen here, but its presence is always felt. The spoor of eland (*Taurotragus oryx*), Cape buffalo and leopard is always evident, and every now and again giant groundsel patches lie like withered carcasses, smashed to pieces by elephants competing with man for the title of the most destructive animal on earth.

There is a deceptive flatness about this area which at first sight would seem to extend as high as the base of the summit peaks. But centuries of glacial activity have slowly eaten away the surface to the extent that the entire region surrounding the peaks has been carved into numerous valleys and gorges, some as deep as 600 m (2,000 ft).

A vast carpet of lobelia and giant groundsel extends over these valleys, clustering thickly along the edges of rivers which flow down them. But for the sounds of these rivers there is a profound silence in the valleys. Malachite sunbirds (*Nectarina famosa*) busily dance around the groundsels, and slender-billed chestnut winged starlings swoop across from boulder to boulder, while overhead the Augur buzzard, Verreaux's eagle and lammergeier hover and wait. Occasionally the silence is shattered by the piercing shriek of the Rock hyrax (*Heterohyrax brucei*), a rabbit-sized animal which inhabits the fissures of rock outcrops and is thought to be a relative of the elephant.

The valleys and gorges of Mount Kenya rise to a point at 4,420 m (14,500 ft) where plants and vegetation give up all attempts to exist. Green turns to grey. Rocks and boulders are suddenly of gigantic proportion, sharper and cruelly angular; then, in turn are broken down into steep scree chutes of pebbles and cinders, rising to the snouts of glaciers and the final vertical 600 m (2,000 ft) of rock and ice, the jewel of Mount Kenya.

Traditionally, mountains are places steeped in legend and folklore. The Carstenz Pyramid, the highest point in Australasia, which rises out of the jungles of New Guinea is one such mountain, while Kangchenjunga, Macha-puchare and Gauri Sankar are good examples of sacred peaks in the Himalayas. Mount Kenya is no exception, and it is not difficult to understand why. Its shimmering snows can be seen from as far as 200 km (120 miles) away by the Wakamba people to the south-east, by the Samburu to the north, and by the Maasai, who roamed over all of southern Kenya in early times. It is interesting to conjecture what this massive formation which glistened white in the equatorial sun must have meant to these people who had never seen or felt snow before. Small wonder that for many it became a source of worship.

For the Kikuyu however, who dwell and farm around the foothills and plains beneath Mount Kenya, their mountain had special meaning, and since the earliest times their lives have been inextricably linked to this often uncompromising peak. It brought them their rain and therefore their livelihood and, during frequent periods of drought, they would pray to it and make sacrifices of lambs and goats. Even today, elder members of the Kikuyu rise early in the morning to offer prayer to Ngai, their god who dwells amongst the summit peaks of Mount Kenya. It is said that by sunrise Ngai will have dispensed all of his blessings upon earlier-rising men.

The story of Ngai and the Gikuyu (changed to Kikuyu in colonial days) is a fascinating one, and in order really to understand Mount Kenya, I feel it is an important one. Nowhere is it better described than by Mzee Jomo Kenyatta (who was to become first president of Kenya in 1963) in his fine book *Facing Mount Kenya*:

> . . . According to tribal legend, we are told that in the beginning of things, when mankind started to populate the earth the man Gikuyu, the founder of the tribe, was called by Ngai (the Divider of the Universe), and was given as his share the land with the ravines, rivers, forests, game and all the gifts that the Lord of Nature bestowed on mankind. At the same time Ngai made a big mountain which he called Kere-Nyaga (Mount Kenya) as his resting place when on inspection tour, and as a sign of his wonders. He then took the man Gikuyu to the top of the mountain of mystery, and showed him the beauty of the country Ngai had given him . . . Before they parted, Ngai told Gikuyu that, whenever he was in need he should make a . . . sacrifice and raise his hands towards Kere-Nyaga . . . and the Lord of Nature would come to his assistance.[1]

Verreaux's black eagle, fierce raptor of the mountain skies.

Superstitions and mystery to this day continue to haunt Mount Kenya. Porters on the mountain have told me that high on the western slopes there is an isolated black-and-white striped cliff with bones littered all about it. Elephants, it is said, would carry encroaching humans to this rock and grind them against it until they had no skin left, then leave the dead and dying at its base. On the eastern moorlands at 3,660 m (12,000 ft) there exists a series of small, rounded mounds, uniformly spaced a few feet apart in parallel lines, graveyard remains perhaps of a vanished race or an ancient battleground of the war-like Mwimbi tribe who used to inhabit these moors.

True or false? It matters little except to those who know their mountain intimately. What can easily be discounted as mere superstition however does often have a way of becoming uncanny reality. Phil Snyder, who used to be the warden of Mount Kenya National Park, told me a story several years ago of how he was interrupted late one evening at his dinner by a group of park rangers. With them was an elderly, barefoot Kikuyu lady carrying a metal plaque from a grave. The rangers had found her alone on the moorlands at 3,960 m (13,000 ft). She had been instructed in a dream to ascend Mount Kenya to the grave of three British climbers[2] who had been killed in an avalanche twenty years before, and remove this plaque from the grave. The voice in the dream had told her that no one who dies on the mountain should be buried there. Now her work was completed, she had no further use for the plaque and she handed it over to Snyder.

There are several interesting questions to ask concerning this incident. How did she know where this grave was? It is located in one of the most inaccessible parts of the peak area, on the screes beneath the Darwin Glacier, a place known only to climbers. What drove her into the Alpine zone with bare feet, clad only in blankets for protection, straight to a point she already knew existed? We shall never know. Snyder never returned the plaque to the grave.

Perhaps the answers to these questions could be given by Ephraim Mk'iara, a

The Mount Kenya Rock Hyrax.

---

[1] Kenyatta, M. J.: *Facing Mount Kenya*; Heinemann Educational (London) 1979.
[2] The accident happened on February 3, 1965; the climbers were Lieutenant Cornish, Corporal Kirkham and Trooper Bunn.

religious zealot from Chogoria, a town at the foot of the eastern slopes of Mount Kenya. Ephraim regularly ascends the mountain in secret . . . "to pray for mankind". There is a slight difference about his ascent however, because he does not simply go to the edge of the glaciers. Ephraim, at the age of 52, wearing only plastic shoes and carrying just a 3-m (10-ft) length of rope, scales the vertical 600-m (2,000-ft) south-east face of Nelion—the mountain's second highest peak at 5,188 m (17,022 ft). He has been known to spend several days on its summit, before descending to his farm. This climb, which is the Normal Route to the summit of Mount Kenya is a very respectable, serious, alpine route, which annually defeats the attempts of countless experienced mountaineers. On his last ascent in 1979, Mk'iara was seen on the summit of Nelion by two British climbers. He is one of the more fortunate of those who ascend to the higher reaches of the mountain for purposes of prayer. Recently the frozen body of another zealot was found on the Lewis Glacier; he had been dead for three months.

On December 3, 1849, Johann Ludwig Krapf became the first white person to see Mount Kenya. Krapf, born in Tübingen, Germany, in 1810, worked for England's Church Missionary Society and had arrived at Mombasa in 1844 with ambitions to establish a chain of mission stations across the continent. Within a few months of arriving both his wife and child had died from malaria, but undaunted he set about his task, and by 1846 the first mission had been built at Rabai, some 20 km (14 miles) inland of Mombasa. There he would translate the New Testament into Swahili.

From Rabai, Krapf made numerous excursions inland, becoming the first explorer to cross Tsavo, and he probed deeply into the country of the Wakamba people. It was from Kivoi, the ruler of the Wakamba, that he first heard rumours of a great mountain mass ". . . the summit of which was covered with a substance resembling white flour", six days' march to the north-west. Cloudy days hindered any chance of seeing the mountain for himself, but finally one morning dawned clear, and from a hill near Kitui he first laid eyes upon ". . . two large horns or pillars, as it were, rising over an enormous mountain to the north-west . . . covered with a white substance".

This "white substance" would prove to be a subject of considerable consternation for Krapf, and his colleague, fellow-missionary Johann Rebmann (see p. 157), who had first sighted Kilimanjaro to the south one year earlier. When word reached the Royal Geographical Society of London of the findings of Rebmann and Krapf, they were met with disbelief and laughter; one esteemed member of the Society, Desborough Cooley, took a vehement stand against the two missionaries, accusing them of being complete frauds. "Calcareous earth" was what they had seen glistening, for snow and ice could not exist so close to the Equator. It was not until 1883 that the Scottish explorer Joseph Thomson sighted the snows of Mount Kenya from Laikipia, and Johann Krapf's word was vindicated.

Four years after Thomson's confirmation of snow on the Equator, an expedition lead by Count Teleki became the first to set foot on the mountain proper. Climbing from the Laikipia Plains, a group was able to penetrate the lower forests and reached an altitude of nearly 4,250 m (14,000 ft) on the south-western moorlands. At this point the expedition was terminated, as the attempt on Mount Kenya had only been a small detour along the route to Lake Rudolf, later re-named Lake Turkana.

In 1893 the first serious attempt to climb Mount Kenya was made. The geologist Dr J. W. Gregory had arrived in East Africa with no intention of climbing the mountain. His expedition was to be one of general geological exploration, but from the beginning it had experienced countless problems,

(*Opposite*) The top of the North Ridge of Mount Kenya and the twin peaks of Batian and Nelion.

Spectacular ice features on the Lewis Glacier, highlighted by the sun.

mainly as a result of uncooperative porters. Upon reaching the Tana River the expedition finally broke down and returned to the coast. Gregory had five months left before having to make his way back to England and he was determined to put his time to good use. He would visit the Rift Valley, the Laikipia plateau and Mount Kenya.

Gregory had already studied a photograph taken by the German explorer Carl Peters, and he knew that his attempt was unlikely to succeed, especially as he would be climbing alone. Nevertheless he felt it was time someone learned more about this space on the map and, with porters from Zanzibar, he attacked the mountain from the south-eastern side. The forest belt proved tougher than he had ever imagined and it took his group four days to reach the edge of the moorlands. Immediately his problems began. The cold drove some of his men back to the lower plains, and those who remained became ill from altitude sickness.

One Zanzibari however stuck by him. His name was Fundi Mabruk, and together they reached the snowline at 4,570 m (15,000 ft). Gregory tried to coax him further with the assistance of a rope but Fundi soon reached a point where he could go no further. Gregory wrote about his porter's reaction to this alien environment: "You'd better come back, master," he sadly cried. "I promised to follow you anywhere in Africa, but how can I when the path stands up on end?"[3] Gregory continued alone, but he too quickly realised that above him stood nearly 600 m (2,000 ft) of vertical grey rock and precariously hanging icefalls. It was no place for a climber on his own. He descended to his porter and then down to their camp.

He now knew that his chances of reaching the summit were remote. The fierce tooth which glittered so tantalisingly in the morning sun seemed to offer no easy way to its tip. Indeed, according to Gregory, there appeared to be no route which would not demand the most advanced European climbing techniques. He therefore decided to make the most of his expedition by climbing onto one of the glaciers. Even this presented its problems:

> I was anxious for an early start next day, and so turned in at sunset, after having in vain tried to persuade Fundi to wear boots and leggings. He tried them on, but flatly refused to wear them; as he also declined to allow me to nail the soles of his feet. I think his hide would have held them.[4]

They reached the Lewis Glacier, and from Gregory's account, he went on alone, probably up to one of the cols between Point Lenana and the south-east face of Nelion. But soon he became altitude sick and was forced back down to his camp. On the following day he received news that his men at a lower camp were ill; he decided that he had given Mount Kenya all he could and ended his expedition.

For a man who was not an experienced mountaineer, the attempt by Gregory was an impressive one. He was the first to enter the Alpine zone, he attained an altitude of about 4,880 m (16,000 ft), and more important, he brought word back of exactly what lay in store for future climbers. In 1894 he wrote a detailed account of his expedition in *The British Alpine Club Journal*, and ended the article: "If this paper should stimulate any members of the father of Alpine Clubs to scale the crags of the highest peak in our African dominions, my paper will have been amply repaid."

This was all that was necessary to fire the imaginations of younger members of the Alpine Club. What followed would be one of the most under-rated journeys of all time, one that never quite received the recognition it was due. During the subsequent hundred years, many more difficult mountains would be climbed, but none would entail problems of the kind experienced by Mackinder along his route to the summit of Mount Kenya.

Halford Mackinder.

Halford Mackinder was studying geography at Oxford University when he read Gregory's article, and heard several of the esteemed geologist's lectures. Although he had no mountaineering experience, there were definite reasons for a fast-developing obsession to scale this remote African peak "because at that time most people would have no use for a geographer who was not an adventurer and explorer". With this in mind, Mackinder set himself an ambitious plan and began the preparations for his expedition which would take place during his long vacation of 1899.

Meanwhile he set aside his long vacation of 1898 to learn everything he could about mountaineering in the European Alps. On this trip he met up with, and was guided by, César Ollier and his young apprentice, Joseph Brocherel. Both these men came from the Italian village of Courmayeur on the south side of Mont Blanc and were amongst the strongest mountaineers of their day. Mackinder lost no time inviting them on his expedition the following year. And so it was that Mackinder's small team of six men gathered in Marseilles during

---

[3] *The British Alpine Club Journal*, 1894.
[4] *ibid.*

the first week of June 1899. With him were C. B. Hausburg, who was to be joint-leader of the expedition and who had shared the expense of it, two biologists, Saunders and Camburn, and Ollier and Brocherel, the latter two being introduced to the sea for the first time! Their ship set sail on June 10 and made a remarkably swift journey, through the Suez Canal, down the Red Sea and East African coast, arriving at Zanzibar on June 28. Here 59 porters were recruited and the expedition sailed on to Mombasa.

Several seasons of rain had failed throughout East Africa and the resultant drought had caused serious food shortages. Barely enough porter food could be found, and Mackinder's problems were compounded by an outbreak of smallpox which extended as far inland as the Uganda border. This necessitated isolating his porters in Mombasa's old Fort Jesus before they could board the train for the 470 km (300 mile) journey inland to the railhead which had reached a decidedly unhealthy spot beside a large swamp called Nairobi.

From the site of Nairobi, Mackinder set off on his 200-km (120-mile) trek to the base of Mount Kenya. His expedition had now grown to 170 men—six Europeans, 66 Zanzibaris and Mombasa Swahilis, 96 Kikuyu, and two Maasai guides. If his problems had appeared insurmountable up until now, Mackinder had seen nothing yet. As the long caravan of men and loads weaved its way across the green hills and valleys of Kikuyu country, food continued to be a major problem, and on one occasion he was forced to hold a village chief hostage until his people produced an adequate amount of food for their requirements. At each village the expedition was met with increasing hostility, and one ambush produced a poisoned arrow which narrowly missed Mackinder himself. If this was not enough, the long drought finally came to an end, and the expedition was grounded by torrential, unseasonal rain, which dampened the general morale of the men and resulted in serious desertions.

On August 19 the men finally reached the base of Mount Kenya, and Ollier and Brocherel immediately set to work cutting a path up through the south-western forest. By following existing elephant trails and keeping high on the ridges, they were able to hack their way through to the moorlands in just one day. This was a considerable achievement in itself, as past attempts had all taken about four days to clear the forest. An intermediate camp was placed at 3,140 m (10,300 ft), and on the following day the two Mont Blanc guides started up across the moorlands into the Höhnel Valley to inspect the peak area of the mountain. Two days later they were back down at camp. The mountain had looked far from easy, but Ollier and Brocherel both felt that it was possible to climb. Everything was finally going well until one member of their party carelessly dropped a lighted match:

> . . . in an instant the grass and groundsel on every side burst into flame. Tree after tree exploded, and as fast as one was extinguished others ignited, till the fire spread ahead of us in a lurid circle, sweeping up the valley and down the mountain slope. Our collecting space, rich with birds and plants, was being denuded before our eyes. For over two hours we fought the fire with our iceaxes, with the result that we eventually stopped it from going up the valley.[5]

Food and provisions continued to be the bane of Mackinder's life. While he and his two guides had been ascending the lower parts of the mountain, he had sent a small expedition under the leadership of Sulimani, the Swahili headman, off to Chief Wangombe's village to restock. The Kikuyu chief gave Sulimani enough food for the porters and suggested that if they required more then they should

---

[5] Mackinder, H., in *Geographical Journal* Vol. XV, 1900.

The South Face of Mount Kenya. The summit of Batian (left) is separated from Nelion by The Gate of the Mists. Below The Gate is the Diamond Glacier joined to the Darwin Glacier below by the ice runnel of the Diamond Couloir.

proceed to the next village. Sulimani sent Sudallah, one of his head porters, and five men, on to find another village, but they had not gone far when they were ambushed by a group lead by Wangombe's own brother. The ensuing fight was a bloody one. Five of the attackers and two of Mackinder's men, including Sudallah, were killed.

The expedition members were able to regroup with Sulimani, who wisely felt it was necessary to withdraw from this area immediately. Although outwardly showing great friendliness, Chief Wangombe had obviously planned the ambush, and Sulimani correctly surmised that another plot was being hatched. They waited until night came, then managed quietly to leave Wangombe's village undetected, and reached Hausburg's camp next morning.

The chronic food problem was therefore unresolved and, to make matters worse, the porter morale reached a new low point after news of the ambush. Hausburg therefore lost no time in arranging for another small expedition to leave for the government station at Naivasha where provisions would be a certainty. However Naivasha lay some 160 km (100 miles) to the west, with the Aberdare Mountains in the way. But there was no alternative, and Saunders was sent along in charge. Now Mackinder's expedition had become a fight against time. The success of the climb would depend upon how quickly Saunders could make the round trip to Naivasha.

All of these happenings had been relayed by letter to Mackinder at his moorland camp. There was little he could do except climb and, with Ollier and Brocherel, he set out on his first attempt on the peak. They made their way up the Teleki Valley then, following Gregory's route, reached the Lewis Glacier, which was crossed to the foot of the South-East Face of Nelion.

Mackinder had named the twin summits of the mountain Batian and Nelion, after Maasai chieftains. Batian, at 5,199 m (17,058 ft) is slightly higher than Nelion, which is 5,188 m (17,022 ft). The peaks are 100 m (300 ft) apart, separated by an icy col which he had called the "Gate of the Mists". The three mountaineers now felt that the easiest way to the summit lay up the vertical 460 m (1,500 ft) South-East Face of Nelion. A descent might then be made into the Gate of the Mists, which looked as though it could be traversed to Batian. The summit of the mountain would then be attempted by climbing directly up from the Gate. It all seemed very possible in theory but Ollier and Brocherel knew from their long years of experience that it would not only be hard, it would be dangerous as well. They were about to begin a climb of major Alpine proportions, the technical difficulties of which started at about the same altitude as the summit of Mont Blanc. This factor alone would make it the most serious climb they had ever undertaken.

A narrow ice couloir (steep ice gully) split the South-East Face of Nelion, and the three climbers correctly reasoned that this would be the fastest way of gaining height on the wall, which was predominantly rock. They cut footsteps up the couloir, Ollier leading out the rope, then the others following, for about one hour, until the ice steepened to such an angle that the rock wall to their left appeared more attractive. Once all three had established themselves on this wall, Ollier was able to piece together in his mind a complicated, but possible route up the 150-m (500-ft) face above. It looked as though good ledge systems could be linked together by a series of more difficult, but shorter, passages which might conceivably lead to Nelion's South-East Ridge. Their judgement was excellent, and with Ollier leading Mackinder, who was the middleman on the rope, Brocherel took up the rear position. Both guides knew that they must succeed in climbing Mount Kenya, but the safety of their client was their first priority.

Slowly they gained altitude up the face. They delighted in the superb quality of the rock, and after the many months of trial and worrying that they had been through, occasionally wondering if they would ever reach the mountain, it was now with considerable relief that they could finally immerse themselves in this vertical world and the climbing of it. Unlike what had gone before, the work ahead was clear; there was risk but it was calculable risk, and this was something they could understand and cope with.

Some 90 m (300 ft) above the glacier, a strenuous chimney was climbed with difficulty. Although the holds were good, every crack was filled with ice and this made progress uncertain. With the chimney behind them, they made faster time and reached the crest of the South-East Ridge just as the sun began to set far over the distant Aberdare Mountains. A sloping ledge was found and the climbers prepared themselves for a long, freezing night. Because of its location on the Equator, the nights on Mount Kenya are virtually twelve hours long, and the three men huddled together for warmth, feeling every second of darkness.

They were now half way up Nelion, and next morning were eager to start moving the moment the sun reached them. The climb continued along the ridge heading for the final 150-m (500-ft) wall of Nelion, the summit of which appeared deceptively close. As Ollier approached the point where the South-East Ridge meets the main face, he was unprepared for the shock he was about to receive. Before him lay an enormous gap, as if a great chunk had been hacked out of the ridge by some giant axe. While Mackinder waited on the ridge, Ollier and Brocherel tried several different ways to climb around this gap, but nothing worked. With heavy hearts the men turned and began the long descent back to the Lewis Glacier, and finally to their camp in the valley.

For César Ollier and Joseph Brocherel their failure to reach the summit, although disappointing, was in a sense to be expected. Mackinder however saw it as a massive set-back. Time was passing too quickly and the worry of exactly what was happening at the base of the mountain weighed on him heavily. He decided to change with Hausburg, and descended to find that Saunders had not yet returned. It was now 15 days since the caravan had set out for Naivasha. All he could do was wait and hope but chances of success were dwindling rapidly.

Meanwhile, 2,440 m (8,000 ft) above him, Hausburg with Ollier and Brocherel had circumnavigated the summit peaks in search of an alternative route, but the western and northern faces of Batian and Nelion appeared to be even more difficult. They had ascended to the summit of the third highest peak, which they named Point Lenana after the chief or *Laibon* of the Maasai, who was Batian's son, but even when viewed from this 4,985-m (16,355-ft) summit, the sheer, eastern faces of Nelion offered no possible route. Finally the Swiss guides decided to attack the steep Darwin Glacier on the mountain's icy South Face, in an effort to gain as much height as possible before being forced onto the uncompromising rock.

All day they cut footsteps up the glacier which reached an angle of 60 degrees. Never had they seen ice this hard to cut and their progress was agonisingly slow. During the afternoon they were so engrossed in the climbing that they failed to notice a storm brewing to the east; by mid-afternoon it lashed them with all the fury of a blizzard. It was a serious predicament, for they could not retrace their steps down and the wind and snow made upward movement impossible. For a while they waited, but the storm, if anything, worsened.

They knew that something had to be done for immobility was now beginning to freeze them. To the east lay the South-East Ridge of Nelion and the point they had reached on their first attempt, and both climbers realised that the ridge was their only chance of survival. Ollier started a long, difficult traverse to the right, while Brocherel played out the rope from his precarious position on the ice-face. It was a situation with no room for error. Eventually Ollier reached some rocks protruding from the ice and was able to secure himself to bring Brocherel across. They were now relatively safe and soon were sitting astride the South-East Ridge of Nelion very close to the point they had reached on their first attempt. There was no discussion this time for they knew they must retreat down the same route as before; both men were completely drained from the storm, and the weather was still uncertain.

Three hours later the storm cleared, and clouds lifted to show a white shimmering peak. As they trudged despondently down the Teleki Valley to their camp the peak was bathed in a rusty alpenglow. It seemed to be laughing at them, safe in the knowledge of its invincibility. At the camp Hausburg awaited them eagerly, and shortly after their arrival handed them the letter which he had received earlier that day. It was from Mackinder. Saunders had not returned and there was no more food. They were to descend. The expedition was over.

The Swiss guides took the news badly. Although the mountain had beaten them twice, they still felt that a route to the summit was possible. To be defeated by a logistical problem at the base of the mountain was unacceptable. Bitterly disappointed, they descended the moorlands and forest with Hausburg, walking in silence and trying to come to terms with failure. They reached camp shortly after dark and what they found was enough to raise their spirits as high as the mountain they could not conquer. Saunders had returned from Naivasha, reaching camp only two hours ahead of them. With him was Captain Gorges, the government officer at Naivasha, and they had brought with them provisions

(Following pages) The East Face of Mount Kenya.

enough for the expedition's march-out, and a little extra for one more attempt on Mount Kenya. It would be the final attempt and this time Mackinder joined Ollier and Brocherel, while Hausburg set off with the main expedition to Naivasha.

Two days later, the climbers reached the head of the Teleki Valley. The tension of this all-or-nothing dash to try to reach the summit of Mount Kenya must have been considerable for the three men, but Mackinder still found time to observe the finer points of being high on a remote mountain:

> The peak was again clear. What a beautiful mountain Kenya is, graceful, not stern, but as it seems to me with a cold feminine beauty. The head of the Teleki Valley with its ruddy cliffs, edged and lined with snow or hail, appears more beautiful in tonight's sunset than ever before. Suddenly the sun must have sunk below the horizon, for the glow went and the whole scene chilled in a moment to an arctic landscape.[6]

On September 12, Mackinder, Ollier and Brocherel left their camp in the Teleki Valley at noon, ascended the moraine of the Lewis Glacier, which they then crossed to the base of the South-East Face of Nelion. They planned this time to follow the route of their first attempt to a point shortly below their previous high-point. From there they intended to traverse across the top of the upper Darwin Glacier, reversing what Ollier and Brocherel had climbed during their stormy second attempt, in an effort to link up with the steep glacier which hangs from the Gate of the Mists between the twin summits.

Progress was fast as they climbed up the difficult chimney and, as light began to fade, they found a good ledge a little below their bivouac on the first attempt and settled down for the night. The morning dawned clear and the climbers were moving as soon as it was light enough to see. From the South-East Ridge they began their traverse across the upper Darwin Glacier.

> But after half an hour it became too steep to climb, and we were obliged to drop on to the hanging glacier to our left which descended from the col between the summits. To cut steps across this glacier direct to the higher summit was the only way left to us. It took three hours to cut our way across this hanging glacier to the farther side of the gap between the two summits, and I gave it the name Diamond Glacier. At first we traversed the ice obliquely upward, each step requiring thirty blows with the axe. There was a thin covering of snow. Then we turned a little towards the base of the lesser summit, but seeing no foothold on the rock we resumed our oblique traverse towards the greater. The Glacier was steep, so that our shoulders were close to it. Had we fallen we should have gone over an ice-cliff on to the Darwin Glacier several hundred feet below.[7]

With the crossing of the Diamond Glacier behind them, the climbers were now established finally on Batian itself, some 90 m (300 ft) below the summit. Above them was a gully which they were able to climb with relative ease, and at noon September 13, 1899 the summit of Mount Kenya was reached for the first time:

> The delay on the glacier had allowed the midday cloud to gather round the peak, but the sun shone through from above, and there were great rifts in the drifting mist through which we looked down on to the glaciers and aretes

[6] Mackinder, H., in *Geographical Journal*, Vol. XV, 1900.
[7] Mackinder, H., *op. cit.*

The view from the huge ice cave under the Diamond Glacier, on the Ice Window Route.

beneath, and away beyond into the valleys radiating from the peak. We remained about forty minutes on the top.[8]

They descended by their route of ascent, leaving the slightly smaller summit, Nelion, unclimbed. It was a long afternoon which extended well into the night, for the last few hundred feet were climbed down in the dark. Camp was reached at 10.20 pm.

For Mackinder and his very able Swiss guides it was the culmination of a long expedition which success had eluded right up until the last moment. César Ollier and Joseph Brocherel would go on to become celebrated mountaineers in Europe, and would return to Africa later to make the first ascents of the highest peaks in the Ruwenzori Mountains. Halford Mackinder would become the pioneer of Geography teaching as we know it today, and was to receive a knighthood. But for all three men, nothing would ever eclipse their moments

---

[8] Mackinder, H., *op. cit.*

together on the top of Mount Kenya when they became the first to stand there. It would be thirty years before anyone else would be able to reach the summit.

With the advent of the twentieth century Kenya changed from a relatively unknown country to one of startling colonial development. The country was young. Farms were struggling and towns were growing. Engineers worked on the railway's descent into the Rift Valley, while architects strived to turn Nairobi from tin to stone. A colony was in the making, and there was little time left for mountain wandering.

In 1908 the glaciers of Mount Kenya were visited by Macgregor Ross and Kermit Roosevelt, but it was not until after World War One that a handful of Kenya's settlers began to explore the moorlands and valleys. A Scottish mission had been built in the village of Chogoria at the base of the eastern slopes of the mountain, and a few of the ministers, no doubt seeking a substitute for their homeland highlands, had walked through the forests and found a world of undulating heather hills and idyllic meadows. Three of the missionaries based at Chogoria were Rev. Dr J. W. Arthur, G. Dennis, and A. R. Barlow. Between them they found a route up through the forest and bamboo, across the sweeping moorlands, and reached the Lewis Glacier. This route from Chogoria became the main way up Mount Kenya, and was later developed by Ernest Carr, a local administrator, who in 1923 built a wooden hut at Urumandi on the moorlands at (3,050 m) (10,000 ft). Carr later drove his Model-T Ford up the Chogoria Track and reached a height of nearly 3,660 m (12,000 ft).

Two other mountain pioneers of the 1920s were E. A. T. Dutton and J. Melhuish. Not only did they hike through hitherto unexplored valleys, but they also had aspirations of reaching the summits. One of their attempts ended on the South-East Ridge of Nelion at a gap which they could not negotiate; on a subsequent attempt Melhuish carried a long wooden ladder for assistance but even this did not help them. They did however make many successful ascents of Point Lenana, and enjoyed skating on a frozen pond beside the Lewis Glacier.

Through people like the missionaries, Dutton, Melhuish and Carr, Mount Kenya gradually became known. Much of it was mapped, and although the summit was never reached, the mountain was enjoyed. In 1929 Dutton wrote *Kenya Mountain*[9], a delightful book which captures brilliantly the atmosphere of the peaks, and the spirit of the day. The enthusiasm of the author for his subject bursts exuberantly from every page.

Helichrysum on the upper Ontulili River, on Mount Kenya's north-western slopes.

In December 1928 a Swiss woman, Vivienne De Watteville, took up temporary residence on the Chogoria Track, basing herself at Urumandi Hut. This was Miss De Watteville's second trip to Africa; her first had been with her father in 1923 when together they had made a collection of the fauna of East Africa for the Berne Museum. One time huntress, now turned naturalist, this trip on her own was primarily aimed at *feeling* Africa, and exploring some of its remoter parts. Mount Kenya therefore proved an irresistible attraction after being described to her by a friend in Nairobi. In her charming book *Speak To The Earth*, she writes:

> It was not merely a single mountain, he told me; it was a whole country of its own and parts of it were unexplored. His descriptions of its wild grandeur, its glaciers and precipices, its valleys full of flowers and its surprisingly blue tarns set down here and there in the wastes of rock, filled me with a longing to be off. However strong the appeal of desert and jungle, the urge of the mountains is strongest of all.[10]

[9] Dutton, E. A. T.: *Kenya Mountain*, Jonathan Cape (London), 1929.
[10] De Watteville, V.: *Speak To The Earth*, Methuen (London), 1935.

After several long discussions with Ernest Carr, Vivienne De Watteville had a good idea of what to expect on the mountain, and with the assistance of Dr Irvine from the Chogoria Mission, she was soon on her way up the forest road with her porters, provisions enough for a two-month stay, and her dog, Siki.

The location of Carr's Urumandi Hut is one of the most beautiful on Mount Kenya, and it seemed the obvious place for the intrepid lady to base herself. Suddenly what had been a stark wooden structure was transformed into a veritable home, and a photograph of its interior in her book shows us an appearance of total feminine neatness, complete with carefully made bed, a bookcase brimming with books, ferns in a pot and a picture on the wall. From Urumandi Vivienne De Watteville made countless sojourns across the moorlands and into the Nithi Gorge—a spectacular deep gash on the mountain's eastern slope through which the Nithi River thunders, at one place cascading over a 60-m (200-ft) cliff, later named Vivienne Falls. Like Dutton before her, it is not difficult to see from the pages of her book the sheer joy and excitement the mountain brought her. Two months alone on any mountain would be enough to tax the hardiest of travellers, but not this woman:

> There was so much to do that the days were never long enough. Besides collecting and painting flowers, exploring the mountain, reading and sketch-

(*Left*) Alpine succulent on Mount Kenya.

(*Above*) Moss and lichen on Mount Kenya.

ing, I wanted to make improvements inside the hut by putting up some more shelves and making curtains for the windows. There was something pleasantly domesticated about sitting in the doorway of an afternoon and sewing away at cretonnes.[11]

As her days of solitude drifted by—all too quickly for her—her perceptions of what the mountain offered heightened to the point where every nuance of light, colour and sound was captured, absorbed, and ultimately stored joyously in her thoughts. Lying on the summit of nearby Mugi Hill, gazing westward at the main peaks of the mountain, she wrote: "Sky and earth brimmed over with rollicking blue; the very wind blowing off the snow sped down on wings of light; the hills danced and the heavens laughed for joy."[12]

One afternoon in the middle of December 1928 the tranquillity of Vivienne De Watteville's home at Urumandi was shattered by the arrival of three young mountaineers and some 20 porters. The climbers set up camp near the hut and, as they sat around the campfire that evening, told her of their plan to climb to the summit of Batian, and also make the first ascent of its twin summit, Nelion. The stories they told fired her imagination and she deeply regretted not having the experience necessary for such a venture. Sharing her fire and dinner that evening were Eric Shipton, Percy Wyn Harris and Gustav Sommerfelt. Shipton's reputation as perhaps the greatest mountain explorer of all time would form in years to come, while Wyn Harris would shortly join a British expedition to attempt the North Ridge of the then unclimbed Mount Everest, and reach an altitude of 8,380 m (27,500 ft) without supplementary oxygen. Here they were together on Mount Kenya and during the following few weeks, the mountain would reverberate to the shock-waves put out by these two young climbers.

Eric Shipton had arrived in Kenya during the rains of October 1928, intent on making Kenya his permanent home. He became an apprentice on a large coffee farm located at Nyeri, 160 km (100 miles) north of Nairobi and close to the base of Mount Kenya. Shipton was only 21 years old, but had already climbed extensively in the Alps. Now situated with Mount Kenya dominating the eastern landscape, he could not take his eyes off it, and eagerly awaited his chance to attempt it.

The chance came in the form of Percy Wyn Harris, who was nearing the end of his first tour as Assistant District Commissioner in one of Kenya's outlying areas. Wyn Harris had also climbed in the Alps, felt he had the necessary ability for a good attempt at the peak, so wrote to Shipton that he was prepared to postpone the date of his sailing back to England by three weeks if Shipton was willing to join him. Shipton jumped at the opportunity and also invited Gustav Sommerfelt along on the trip. Sommerfelt, an old friend of Shipton's, was another budding coffee farmer and, although totally inexperienced as a climber, possessed an easy-going, optimistic personality which Shipton felt would enhance the expedition.

The climbers left Vivienne De Watteville to her peaceful retreat, and moved up the Chogoria Track to the edge of the Lewis Glacier. Their plan was initially to attempt Mackinder's Route, but during their approach across the moorlands the North-East Face of Batian had continually been in their sight and had impressed them as having great potential. On the afternoon of the day they reached the snow-line, Shipton and Wyn Harris immediately set off to reconnoitre the North-East Face:

---

[11] De Watteville, V., *op. cit.*
[12] De Watteville, V., *op. cit.*

We were delighted to find that the rock was as firm and clean-cut as Chamonix granite, and though we climbed several hundred feet up it, we found nothing to chasten our confidence. Night was falling as we scrambled back to our camp up the scree slope, our lungs bursting and our spirits high. The weather was fine, and neither of us doubted that, the very next day, the summit of Batian would be reached for the second time, after a lapse of thirty years.[13]

Eric Shipton.

Next day, accompanied by Sommerfelt, they made their bid for the summit but, several hundred feet above their previous high-point, they were brought up against an unclimbable overhanging section of the face. Mount Kenya was not going to give in this easily, and the three climbers descended and returned to camp.

Shipton and Wyn Harris lost no time in redirecting their plans to Mackinder's Route, and on the following day inspected the South-East Face of Nelion. This looked very difficult, particularly in its upper section, and on the morning of January 6, 1929, their morale low, the two climbers moved across the Lewis Glacier to the base of the climb. Once on the route however, things appeared more promising and they moved with incredible speed up the difficult chimney, from which still hung Mackinder's old frayed rope. By 8.30 am they were established on the South-East Ridge of Nelion. The day was clear and they could see Kilimanjaro rising above the clouds 400 km (250 miles) to the south.

Instead of traversing leftwards across the top of the upper Darwin Glacier, as Mackinder had, Shipton and Wyn Harris decided to try and climb Nelion direct. This would mean overcoming the obstacle which had defeated Mackinder's first attempt, and they descended into the gap which had ended Ollier's hard work. Shipton tried to climb straight up but this proved impossible, while an attempt to the left met with a similar lack of success. Finally he moved around to the right along a narrow ledge which took him to an exposed position over the 300-m (1,000 ft) vertical East Face of Nelion:

> There, poised over a sheer drop, I came upon a shallow crack which split the wall above. It was not wide enough for me to wedge my foot, and the only holds were smooth and outward sloping, but it was clearly the only way. My movements were very slow, and at each upward step I expected to find another progress blocked. At last, sixty feet above the cleft, I reached a comfortable stance with a good belay. The pitch had taken more than an hour to accomplish.[14]

Above, it looked equally intimidating and Shipton suggested to Wyn Harris that they abandon the attempt and look for another way, but Wyn Harris was emphatic that this route be pursued, and so they continued. A narrow gully which they had not seen from below provided a path through a band of overhangs above and the key to Nelion. It was nearly noon when they reached the 5,188-m (17,022-ft) hitherto unclimbed summit. After a short rest, they descended into the Gate of the Mists, crossed this icy col and moved up onto Batian. At 1.30 pm, they reached the summit of Mount Kenya. It had been an excellent climb, brilliantly executed, but there was little time for rest. Much ground had to be covered in the descent and they started down immediately. They retraced their steps back to the summit of Nelion then roped down to the South-East Ridge without difficulty. By nightfall they were safely at the foot of

---

[13] Shipton, E.: *That Untravelled World*, Hodder and Stoughton (London), 1969.
[14] Shipton, E., *op. cit.*

the climb. It was only six days since Shipton and Wyn Harris had set out from Nairobi.

Two days later Vivienne De Watteville approached the edge of the Lewis Glacier when she heard voices calling from high above:

> I quickened my pace, looking curiously ahead, but the voices came no nearer. And then by chance I raised my eyes to the peak, and there, standing on the topmost summit, were three figures diminutive as ants. So crystal clear was the air that their voices, not raised above ordinary conversational tones, had come down to me nearly fifteen hundred feet below.[15]

Shipton and Wyn Harris had repeated their climb, this time with the novice Sommerfelt. That evening they were back at their camp, now shared with the indomitable lady. She describes meeting the climbers after their return from the peak:

> What impressed them most was Mackinder's courage. They said that they would have tackled any kind of rock rather than go the way he went, crossing that perilously canted stretch of ice hanging over the void.
>
> I put a hundred questions; but even in that uplifting moment of achievement they continually drew the talk away from themselves and back to Mackinder.[16]

The weather broke soon after the ascent with Sommerfelt. With time running out, and Wyn Harris with a ship to catch, the expedition descended, leaving Mackinder's "monarch of mountains" and a woman with her flowers.

[15] De Watteville, V., *op. cit.*
[16] De Watteville, V., *op. cit.*

(*Opposite*) A view from the summit of Nelion, looking towards Point John.

The West Face of Mount Kenya.

Climbing the knife-edge North-East Ridge of Point Dutton.

When viewed from the north or south, the beautifully serrated West Ridge of Batian holds the eye of the mountaineer longer than any other feature. It is a finely chiselled skyline worthy of the proudest of mountains and it was to this that Eric Shipton next set his sights:

> Few mountains have such a superb array of ridges and faces. From the summit of Batian a sharp, serrated crest runs northwards for some distance before plunging steeply to the north-east, the other descending westward in a series of huge steps to a col dividing Batian from a massive peak known as Point Piggot. This was the ridge that we hoped to climb. The largest of the steps appeared to be some five hundred feet high and vertical; I called it the Grand Gendarme, a name it still bears. Below was the Petit Gendarme, a pinnacle standing above the col at the foot of the ridge. The West Ridge was obviously a formidable proposition . . .[17]

Shipton was correct in his assumption. It would be a formidable undertaking, but at the end of it he would have what could be called the classic mountaineering route of Mount Kenya; indeed it would be difficult to find a grander climb on the African continent.

For the attempt Shipton was accompanied by another young, struggling farmer from western Kenya, H. W. Tilman. Bill Tilman had done some

---

[17] Shipton, E., *op. cit.*

rock-climbing in England's Lake District, and had more recently, with
Shipton, ascended both Kibo and Mawenzi on Kilimanjaro, but for a route like
the West Ridge he was remarkably inexperienced. This would however be ably
compensated for by his extraordinary drive and energy.

This time Shipton approached the peaks from the western side, using
pack-mules provided by a farmer, Raymond Hook, who lived at the base of the
mountain. This journey took them up into the Mackinder Valley from where
they were able to see the West Ridge in all its detail. For acclimatisation
purposes, and in order to study the lower aspect of the ridge they made the
first ascents of Point Peter, 4,757 m (15,608 ft) and Point Dutton, 4,885 m

Mackinder Valley lava cave near the
peaks of Tereri and Sendeyo.

Walter Treibel stands on the small tooth below the summit of Point Peter.

(16,028 ft), two fine spires which are attached to the lower part of the West Ridge.

Next day they reconnoitred the approach up the Joseph Glacier to the notch at the base of the ridge. Good steps were cut up the ice and by midday they were astride the knife-edge crest of the col, staring up at a totally intimidating prospect. Through boiling clouds they could see up the ridge as far back as the Grand Gendarme, but as Tilman later wrote: "What lay beyond we could not tell, and it seemed doubtful whether we should get far enough to learn."[18]

At 4.30 am on the following morning the two climbers departed from their camp at the head of the Mackinder Valley, leaving the cave which would later bear Shipton's name, and with staggering speed attained their previous high-point by 8.00 am. With such a mammoth task ahead of the climbers it would seem somehow fitting to describe a detailed, epic struggle during this first ascent of the West Ridge of Mount Kenya. Countless modern mountaineers have been defeated by the technical problems and sheer length of the climb, but Shipton and Tilman climbed it with masterly skill and in a time which few modern parties with sophisticated equipment have been able to achieve since. They traversed the south side of the Petit Gendarme, then the north side of the Grand Gendarme. Above this they reached the foot of what would provide the crux of their climb and, in turn, the key to the West Ridge. Shipton, who led the entire route, writes:

> When I looked at the next obstacle, however, my optimism dissolved. This was a step, reddish in colour, 130 feet high, extremely steep and undercut at its base.
>
> This time there was no way of turning it: to the right was a giddy drop to the hanging glaciers of the west face, to the left the scoop at the base of the step continued as a groove, running obliquely downwards across the north face, overhung by a continuous line of ice-polished slabs. By standing on Bill's shoulders I could just reach two finger holds; hanging on there, with a final kick off my companion's head, I managed to hoist myself up to grasp a hold higher up, and also to find some purchase with my feet to relieve the strain on my arms. The wall above the scoop was nearly vertical, and the holds were only just large enough for a boot nail; but, though few, they were well spaced and the rock was sound . . .[19]

All this was taking place at about 5,120 m (16,800 ft), but Shipton surmounted the obstacle and was able to pull the rope tightly enough to enable the inexperienced Tilman to overcome the difficulties. From this point there was no stopping the climbers, and they hastily moved along the remaining ridge to the summit of the mountain which was reached at 4.30 pm. Now Shipton was on familiar ground and, with less than three hours of daylight left, they crossed the Gate of the Mists to Nelion. As they started down the South-East Face, Tilman fell but was held on the rope by his companion; his ice-axe however disappeared over the edge of Nelion falling over 300 m (1,000 ft) to the Darwin Glacier far below. Shipton knew this face better than anyone and, after a short wait for the moon to rise, they abseiled down in its glow, reaching the safety of the Lewis Glacier at 9.00 pm.

It was a phenomenal achievement, this first complete traverse of the summit of Mount Kenya by two of the greatest mountain adventurers of all time. Shipton wrote: "Bill had been magnificent; he had shown no sign of anxiety throughout the climb, and his stoicism no less than his innate skill in climbing

(*Opposite*) Point John reflected in Hut Tarn.

[18] Tilman, H. W.: *Snow on the Equator*; Macmillan (London), 1938.
[19] Shipton, E., *op. cit.*

Point Peter.

and handling the rope made a vital contribution to our success."[20]

This was the beginning of what would unfold into a career of countless achievements for Tilman. It would take him to Mount Everest, and later to make the first ascent of 7,817 m (25,645 ft) Nanda Devi, the highest climbed mountain at that time. Like Shipton, he would become a cult-figure respected by all those inclined towards the outdoors.

The successes of 1929 and 1930 on Mount Kenya immortalised Eric Shipton as the finest climber of his generation, and he was solely responsible for placing the mountain firmly on the map. In a short period of time he had made the second ascent of Batian, the first ascent of Nelion, the first ascent of the magnificent West Ridge of Batian and, with various partners, had pioneered the ascents of many of the mountain's outlying peaks including Point John, Midget Peak, Point Pigott, Point Dutton, Point Peter and Tereri.

His ascent of the West Ridge would be the hardest technical problem he would ever encounter. After Mount Kenya he would drift more towards mountain exploration in other ranges and establish himself as the greatest mountain explorer of all time, a vehement advocate of light-weight, small expeditions. He would be responsible for finding the route of least resistance to the summit of Mount Everest, but was to relinquish at the last moment the leadership of the eventual first ascent when the expedition became too large and public a venture.

The three men crept through the rain forest cautiously, senses alerted for the slightest unusual sound. There was a melodramatic strangeness to their move-

[20] Shipton, E., *op. cit.*

ments which verged on comedy, as the man at the rear of the line, in his efforts to look behind him, continually stumbled noisily, much to the irritation of his companions. Fear exuded from this man whose every action acknowledged the fact that he was far from his natural environment, and contrasted sharply with the demeanour of his two friends. In their eyes was an almost maniacal determination to put this forest, and everything which lay beneath it, as far behind them as possible. For Felice Benuzzi and Giovanni Balletto any obstacle this mountain threw in their path, including the rhino earlier that morning, was infinitely preferable to what they had escaped from. Enzo Barsotti was not so sure, but he knew what this meant to his companions—both mountaineers from their distant home in Italy. No matter what lay before him, he would not let them down.

It was 1943 and the world was at war. Even remote Somalia had been caught up in the chaos. Italians taken prisoner there by the British had been transported across the southern border into the British colony of Kenya. Many were interned in war camps across the country, some to be sent out daily to work as labourers on neighbouring farms, others to the railway yards and factories in Nairobi. One prison had been erected close to the town of Nanyuki, which lay beneath the western foothills of Mount Kenya and it was upon this barbed-wire encampment that an unusual story focused.

It would be difficult for anyone who has not spent time in a prisoner-of-war camp to understand completely the full implications and the effect on the individual's self-esteem of the sudden curtailment of freedom. The British prison camps in Kenya were "camps" only in the loosest sense of the word. None of the cruelty and injustices now associated with those in Europe at that time existed in Kenya, but the confinement and the barbed-wire did.

Compounding the withdrawal of this freedom was the very country itself. Kenya epitomises everything that is "outdoors". It is a land of space and sky, and for a mountaineer such as Felice Benuzzi, to be interned beneath Mount Kenya was unmitigated torture. Each morning as he stared up at its snows, it was like salt rubbing into his already considerable wound. A permanent escape from the camp was unrealistic for there was nowhere to escape to. The duration of the war would have to be spent in the camp, but life even just a few yards on the other side of the wire would have been tolerable for him. Later, in his very readable book *No Picnic On Mount Kenya*, he would write:

> If there is no means of escaping to a neutral country or of living under a false name in occupied Somalia as many have done, then, I thought, at least I shall stage a break in this awful travesty of life. I shall try to get out, climb Mount Kenya and return here.[21]

Weeks of preparation followed:

> The more I considered the idea of escape, the more I realised the magnitude of the task I had set myself. Should we be able to climb without a long period of acclimatisation in the thin air of 17,000 feet? How should we make the actual climb? Whom should I ask to accompany me? How could we get out of camp and in again? These and other problems kept my mind fully occupied. I found it fascinating to elaborate, in the utmost secrecy, the first details of my scheme.
>
> Life took on another rhythm because it had a purpose.[22]

---

[21] Benuzzi, F.: *No Picnic on Mount Kenya*, William Kimber (London), 1952.
[22] Benuzzi, F., *op. cit.*

Mawenzi, seen from the North Ridge.

followed later by Mawenzi. Kibo, geologically speaking, is recent and wit-
nessed most of its activity during the Pleistocene period. It is possible however
that the last major episode of activity took place within the last few centuries.

As with the other mountains of eastern and central Africa, there are definite
vegetational zones on Kilimanjaro. A complete thick belt of montane forest
encircles the entire mountain between 1,900 m and 3,000 m (6,200 ft and
9,800 ft), and is dominated by *Podocarpus* trees which are of giant proportions
with buttressed roots. Cedar trees also grow in profusion on the lower northern
slopes, often festooned with thick, woody lianes. An array of large ferns and
nettles makes passage in the forest difficult but, unlike other high mountains in
Africa, virtually no bamboo exists on Kilimanjaro.

The forest is a silent place and although it is inhabited by mammals they are
not present in the numbers which can be seen on Mount Kenya. Elephant and
Cape buffalo are the most common larger animals of the forest, while bushbuck
and duiker (*Cephalophus spadix*) can also be seen, but the chances of the visitor
either seeing or hearing any of them, or even noticing so much as a sign of them,
are remote. Colobus monkeys are probably the most likely wildlife to be spotted
on Kilimanjaro.

Above the forest lie the moorlands between 2,750 m and 4,270 m (9,000 ft
and 14,000 ft). On the northern slopes forests of heather grow in abundance,
while to the south it is gentler, more undulating country carpeted by tussock
grass and occasional clumps of giant groundsel and lobelia.

In the higher regions of the mountain there are few deep sheltered valleys and
the slopes consist of very porous lavas. Therefore the little water that falls as rain
or descends as melt-water from the glaciers does so underground for long

distances and is virtually unavailable to plants. As a result the flora on Kilimanjaro is very poor when compared with other East African mountains.

The spoor of leopard can often be seen on the trails of the upper moorlands and Alpine zone, while the piercing shriek of the Rock hyrax often shatters the tranquillity of the mountain day. For many years The Saddle has boasted a large herd of eland whose fur is long, making them appear larger than their shorter-haired, lowland counterparts.

Between April and June 1848, Johann Rebmann, a missionary working for the Church Missionary Society, was travelling across the plains of Tsavo in what would later be known as south-eastern Kenya. Rebmann was from Germany, born in January 1820 in Gerlingen, and had, since June 1846, been based at the mission station Rabai, near Mombasa. Also at Rabai was Johann Krapf (see p. 126), and in an effort to spread the gospel further than the coastal region the missionaries often travelled inland, becoming the first white people to set foot on the country they crossed. The purpose of Rebmann's 1848 journey was to penetrate the land of the Wachagga people to see if there might be potential for the setting up of a mission station.

On the morning of May 11, 1848 his caravan neared the town of Taveta, and he saw ahead of him that the plains ended, giving way to a country of green, rolling hills rising ever higher into the clouds: ". . . at about ten o'clock I thought I saw one of them enveloped in a prominent white cloud. My guide

(*Below left*) Crater rim on Kibo, and the Eastern Icefields.

(*Below*) Moorland on Kilimanjaro.

simply described the whiteness that I saw as cold [*baridi*]; and it was as good as certain to me that it could be nothing else other than snow."[1]

Despite attempts by Rebmann to describe to his party the meaning of *snow*, it was something they could not understand. One guide however knew there was a strangeness about the substance, and told the missionary that once when he was passing through this area he had dispatched several porters up the mountain with instructions to bring back as much of the "silver" as they could carry. However, they returned a few days later with only water, much to the disappointment of the waiting caravan.

As with his colleague Johann Krapf who would first see the snows of Mount Kenya in 1849, Rebmann's claim to have seen ice on Kilimanjaro was rebuffed by the Royal Geographical Society in London. In Germany however, the description of this giant ice-capped peak in Africa must have fired the imagination for it became an obsession of the country, and would inextricably link the Germans with the early history of Kilimanjaro.

Thirteen years later the first Kilimanjaro expedition was launched from Zanzibar under the leadership of the German adventurer Baron Carl Claus von der Decken. Accompanied by a young British geologist, Richard Thornton, and a caravan of more than 50 porters, the expedition set off from Mombasa on June 29, 1861. The Baron crossed the Taru Desert and Taita district, encountering along the route considerable opposition from various tribal leaders who demanded compensation for the right to cross their territory. Each obstacle was however taken in their stride and on July 14, 1861 the explorers laid eyes upon Kilimanjaro. Shortly afterwards von der Decken and Thornton reached the base of the mountain, but the constant haggling with local chiefs together with growing dissension amongst the porters ended the attempt in the middle of the lower forest belt. The expedition did however spend 19 days on the lower slopes and Thornton was able to estimate the mountain as between 6,040 m and 6,300 m (19,812 ft and 20,655 ft), concluding it was a volcano.

In November 1862 Baron von der Decken mounted a second expedition to Kilimanjaro. This time he took with him Dr Otto Kersten, a young German scientist. Although the mountain again defeated the Baron, it allowed him to attain an altitude of nearly 4,000 m (13,100 ft) where, to his delight, he experienced the next best thing to reaching the summit—a fall of snow.

Upon his return to Zanzibar in March 1863 Baron von der Decken met a missionary from the United Methodist Free Churches of England called Charles New. The Baron's tales of Kilimanjaro inspired the 23-year-old man to see this mountain for himself, but his work near Mombasa at the Ribe Mission was to keep him busy until 1871. New's reason for visiting the mountain was simple and surprisingly far-sighted: Europeans could not colonise East Africa from a base on the unhealthy coastal plain. A more moderate climate typical of a higher altitude was required, and perhaps Kilimanjaro and its region would offer the perfect location.

Charles New reached the slopes of the mountain in July 1871. His first major obstacle awaited him near the town of Moshi in the form of Mandara, the Wachagga chief. Mandara was demanding, conniving and totally unpredictable. The missionary had arrived prepared with presents for the chief but they were too few; he persevered, trying to secure the chief's goodwill, but it did not come to anything. As to New's intention of ascending Kilimanjaro, Mandara was uncompromising: "Who are you that you should ascend the mighty Kilima Njaro? Haven't our people tried it again and again without success? Didn't the last Mzungu (European) that came here try it, and wasn't he driven back?"[2]

[1] Rebmann, Jo: Dispatches; *The Church Missionary Intelligences*, Vol. 1, No. 1 (May 1949).
[2] New, C.: *Life, Wanderings and Labours in Eastern Africa*; Macdonald (London), 1971.

Desert and ice contrast on the edge of Kibo Crater.

Mandara did not turn out to be God's answer to New's problems involving porter morale:

> Then we were told all manner of fabulous stories about the supernatural occupants of the mountain's summit, who were watching over immense hoards of gold, silver, and precious stones, and who would treat in the most summary manner any mortal daring to enter upon their sacred domains. We were informed of parties venturing too far up the mountain, who were so effectually disposed of that they were never seen again; of others who returned with frost-bitten limbs, telling the most frightful stories of their experiences. Mandara gave us an account of a passage he had made of the mid-portion of the mountain on his way to Rombo and Useri. Such was the weather he encountered, that despite his best endeavours he lost no less than fifteen men in one day.[3]

New made one attempt on the peak but was forced back by bad weather before he had climbed through the forest. A second attempt in August met with greater success and he reached The Saddle, becoming the first man to touch snow on Kilimanjaro when he found it ". . . lying on ledges of rock in masses, like large sleeping sheep".[4]

In 1875 New returned to the mountain but this time Mandara stripped him

[3] New, C., *op. cit.*
[4] New, C., *op. cit.*

(*Following pages*) Kibo, and evening light on the Decken and Reibmann glaciers, from the south-east.

Protea species on Kilimanjaro.

bare of all his possessions. His spirit broken, the missionary turned for home; he became ill and died before reaching Mombasa.

Some years later the Scottish explorer Joseph Thomson journeyed to the Kilimanjaro region and half-heartedly climbed to about 2,440 m (8,000 ft) on the south-eastern slopes. He met Mandara and traded him his personal tweeds and double-barrelled gun; in return he received the gold watch which the wily chief had extracted from Charles New eight years previously.

If the friendliness and sincerity of Charles New and Joseph Thomson had been misinterpreted by Mandara as weakness, the Chief of the Wachagga was about to meet his match in the form of Harry Johnston. Johnston, a 26-year-old naturalist, was sent to the Kilimanjaro area in charge of a scientific expedition to collect and describe the flora and fauna. Sponsoring this six-month-long journey were the British Association for the Advancement of Science, the Royal Society and the Royal Geographical Society, but it is marginally possible that there might have been an ulterior motive. John Kirk, the British Consul in Zanzibar had repeatedly expressed to his government that time should not be lost in securing complete control of East Africa: "We cannot expect to go on for long as we have done. If we hesitate, some other Power, less scrupulous, may step in and forestall us. The French priests are very desirous that France should move here . . . The Belgian International Association has ideas that cross the whole continent . . . There are mysterious Germans travelling inland and a German man-of-war is reported on the coast . . ."[5]

The expedition of Joseph Thomson in 1883 was a direct result of Kirk's requests but, much to the detriment of the consul and the explorer, Thomson found himself following the recent footsteps of a German expedition under the leadership of Dr Gustav Fischer across the Kilimanjaro region. Because of this Thomson quickly shifted his ambitions further north to what is now modern-day Kenya, and perhaps inadvertently initiated the delineation of future boundaries and interests.

Kirk, however, was still vehemently for British control of Kilimanjaro, and Harry Johnston's expedition at the time was rumoured to be a major step in this direction. Johnston was tough, flamboyant, a little eccentric and very ambitious. Despite his youth he had already travelled across Tunisia, explored Angola, and met Stanley in the Congo. He stood to gain much from this Kilimanjaro quest and nothing would stand in his way. In early May 1884, accompanied by 30 Zanzibari porters and a letter of introduction from Kirk, Johnston reached Moshi and literally swept Mandara off his feet with charm and an impressive array of effective presents. His arrival was also timely, for Mandara was having problems with neighbouring tribes and a minor state of civil war was developing; Johnston took full advantage of this. Ever unpredictable, the chief's attitude would change from day to day, but Johnston lost no time in procuring some land from him, establishing a base at Kitimbiriu near Moshi. Here he built several huts including a three-roomed cottage for himself. From here Johnston conducted numerous *safaris* in the area, hunting and collecting. In October he made a concerted attempt on the peak and later reported that he reached an altitude of 5,973 m (16,315 ft)—a claim that has been questioned. At the end of the month he descended and returned to Zanzibar. His work in the area would later secure him a knighthood from Queen Victoria.

The initial exploratory period of Kilimanjaro came to an end with the climbs of Professor Hans Meyer, a Leipzig geographer, who made his first attempt to reach the summit of Kibo in August 1887. It was a worthy try, reaching approximately 5,180 m (17,000 ft), and probably would have succeeded if his

[5] Kirk, J.: British Consul in Zanzibar in 1880s suggests scientific expedition to Kilimanjaro.

Inside Kibo Crater—the inner Reusch Crater, ashpit and Western Terrace.

companion, Baron von Eberstein, had not become seriously ill with altitude sickness. A second attempt in July 1888 was called to an abrupt halt in the Usumbara Mountains, when Hans Meyer's caravan of 230 porters was caught up in an Arab rising against the German-East Africa Society's attempts to depose Islamic rule on the coast. Although his expedition was well inland, some tribes sympathised with the revolt of the coastal people, including Chief Sembodja of Masinde. Hans Meyer's caravan was intercepted at the town of Kihuiro, broken up, and all of his supplies seized. He returned despondently to Zanzibar.

The professor was not yet ready to give up and in August 1889 he once again returned to East Africa, this time with Ludwig Purtscheller. Purtscheller was perhaps the most distinguished alpinist of his day and had successfully climbed the major summits in the European Alps. This time the base of Kilimanjaro was reached without mishap on September 24 and four days later they started up the mountain. By now the route to The Saddle was fairly clear and it took the expedition just five days to gain the base of Kibo. Hans Meyer and Purtscheller began the final climb at 1.00 am on October 3 and their route took them up the eastern, scree-carpeted slopes of Kibo to the base of the lowest glacier which was reached at 9.50 am. At this point, crude crampons and axes helped them gain height up the ice and at 2.00 pm they became the first men to look into the crater of Kibo. They were at an altitude of 5,670 m (18,600 ft) and they could see the highest point of Kilimanjaro standing almost 300 m (1,000 ft) higher on the far south-western edge of the crater rim. There was little time left and the climbers descended to their camp.

After one day of rest, the two Germans started up again, but this time a night was spent in a cave which Hans Meyer had previously discovered at 5,182 m

(17,000 ft). This gave them a good early start on the following day and at 8.45 am the crater's edge was reached. The climbers then moved slowly around the crater rim and at 10.30 am Hans Meyer became the first person to stand on the highest point of Africa. It was also the highest point in the German Empire and he named it Kaiser Wilhelm Spitze.

Hans Meyer and Purtscheller were far from satisfied with their considerable achievement of having reached the summit of Kilimanjaro, and now directed their attentions to the unclimbed Mawenzi, which would prove an even more formidable adversary. Mawenzi, at 5,148 m (16,894 ft), is in many ways a mountain in its own right; but there is one major difference between it and its more approachable sister Kibo—the top is guarded by sheer rock walls on all sides. No walking route exists to the summit of Mawenzi. There is something wonderfully appealing about this bruised old peak; it is as though it tries to be everything which Kibo is not. In no way has it been influenced by the graceful symmetry of the taller peak and in place of the glorious snow-dome, we have a confusion of sheer rock spires rising several hundred feet above The Saddle —tarnished yet supreme in its complexity. An old Wachagga legend says that once, in ancient times, when both were still smoking their pipes, that of Mawenzi became extinguished. He went to his bigger but younger brother, Kibo, to borrow fire, and received it. A short time later, while taking a nap, the fire in his pipe again went out. And again he went to borrow from Kibo. But this time the latter became very angry and thrashed him so terribly with his club that even now one can see its bruised, battered and torn surface and sense its attitude of austerity, adopted after this unjust treatment. The Wachagga believe that Mawenzi is ashamed of its appearance, therefore covering its face with clouds at every opportunity. This is a little unfair as the peak can look very impressive, but what is interesting about the legend is the accurate description of the volcanic history of the mountain. The Wachagga have obviously existed beneath Kilimanjaro for many centuries.

Between October 13 and 22, 1889, Hans Meyer and Purtscheller made three attempts to scale Mawenzi but all were in vain. The climbers were amazed by just how technical the climbing was, and the highly competent Purtscheller had never climbed anything as serious as this before. They eventually decided that Mawenzi's untrodden summit would have to wait for a future expedition, and the two Germans rounded off their successful trip by making two further rapid ascents of Kibo, one from the north and the other from the east. It would not be until July 29, 1912 that two German climbers, E. Oehler and F. Klute, would make the first ascent of Mawenzi.

I first saw Kilimanjaro in March 1959 when I was 11 years old, when my parents and I were travelling between Arusha in northern Tanzania and the Kenyan border town of Namanga. As my father's little Morris 1000 made its way northward round the shoulder of Mount Meru, I gazed out of the back window, my eyes transfixed by the 4,565-m (14,978-ft) volcano which loomed over us, frozen against the landscape. As I looked beyond Meru I became aware of something rising large and white above the distant plains, until there was no doubt in my mind as to what I was looking at. It was not just the shimmering snow-dome of Kibo rising through the dust which took my breath away, but the sheer immensity of the entire mass which stood before me. It was one of the great moments of my life and I promised myself that one day I would climb it.

Three years later, when I was 14, I made my first step towards Kilimanjaro when I was able to attach myself to a small party of students who planned to climb Mount Meru. Wrong mountain but right direction. The ascent went well for me as I was one of the few who did not become ill with the altitude and, climbing alone, I reached the top shortly before daybreak on the third day of

(*Opposite*) Mawenzi—the North Face from Mawenzi Tarn.

Wind-blown snow near Stella Point on the edge of Kibo Crater.

Kilimanjaro from Mount Meru, fifty kilometres away.

the climb. It was clear and cold and I sat on Meru's fine summit, gazing eastward down across the broken caldera and over to Kilimanjaro with the sun beginning to rise behind it. I felt as if I could have stretched out and caressed its glinting snows. Obviously it had to be next.

One year later the opportunity arose when my school in Nairobi decided to arrange an expedition to ascend what was now known as the Tourist Route and, although slightly under-age, my name was soon on the list of aspiring candidates. By now the trail up Kilimanjaro had become fairly popular and two hotels had been built at the base of the mountain to cater for the increasing number of people who came each year to try their luck. We camped in the grounds of the Marangu Hotel and very quickly found ourselves caught up in an atmosphere of wonderful anticipation about what the following five days might bring.

Kilimanjaro burst out of every shadow in the old hotel. Here lay an ice-axe in a corner, while over there someone had left an old woollen balaclava and snowgoggles. Ancient sepia photographs of Kibo and Mawenzi hung from every wall, while climbers sat ponderously at tables or lounged in comfortable armchairs. There was an obvious distinction between those who were about to climb and those who had just returned. The former, pale-faced and worried, could barely relax; questions tumbled around in their minds. How cold will it be? What will the weather be like? Do I have enough clothing? Will I be able to keep up with my friends? And perhaps the major concern . . . will I manage to elude the dreaded mountain sickness which seems to affect so many? The latter group, faces burned to a stretched crisp, lips swollen, hungry and, whether they had succeeded or not, content that it was behind them. With my pale face and concerned thoughts, I decided to retire to my tent early and spent a long night seeking sleep which refused to oblige.

Our route up the mountain lay clearly ahead of us. On the first day we hiked

up through the rain forest to Bismark Hut at approximately 2,740 m (9,000 ft). This old stone structure, built before World War One, was where we would spend the night, and from its cobbled verandah I could look down over the plains of Kenya to Lake Chala and the sprawling Lake Jipe. Next day felt more as if we were now truly on the mountain, as the narrow path traversed the southern moorlands. The walking between each hut was to take about five hours and, as we approached Peter's Hut on our second day, many of us began to feel the effects of the altitude. This hut, another stone building, is located at 3,660 m (12,000 ft). Situated well above the forest edge, surrounded by miles of short *Erica* bush, Peter's Hut has a windswept feel about it, but there are compensations. Directly behind us stood the craggy Mawenzi, while above and over to our left was Kibo, its considerable ice fields glowing orange in the setting sun.

On our third day we hiked slowly up towards The Saddle. The going was no longer easy, and for some who had experienced a bad night, it was a tough walk. We traversed over the south-western shoulder of Mawenzi and reached The Saddle at midday. The Saddle is about as close as one can come to walking on the moon and must be one of the strangest places on earth. A massive brown sweep of high-altitude desert guarded by Mawenzi to the east and Kibo to the west. From The Saddle, Kibo is no longer as impressive, but the lofty sentinel of Mawenzi stands forth totally capturing the eye and imagination. For the hiker, The Saddle brings relief; several hours are spent walking across its flat surface, and only during the final hour when the path subtly rises to Kibo Hut does one begin to realise that 4,700 m (15,420 ft) has been reached.

Not a great deal can be said for the location of this final hut on the way to the summit of Kilimanjaro. It is desolate and cold and the majority of walkers are in no mood to enjoy any small pleasures which the district might offer. Headaches

Ice-cliffs on Kilimanjaro's north-east side.

and nausea are being nursed by many of the hut's occupants and most people are thoroughly intimidated by the prospect of the final 920 m (3,000 ft) of scree, a climb which will begin at 1.00 am the following morning. There are good reasons for starting at this early hour. The scree, which is comprised of small, pebble-like ash cinders is frozen then and is therefore easier to climb; when the sun rises it does so from behind Mawenzi, beautifully illuminating the serrated silhouette of this peak—the higher one is up the Kibo scree by the time the sun rises, the grander the view. But for many the third reason for beginning so early is the one which makes the greatest sense: it is dark and therefore one cannot see the vast distances ahead, which in daylight never seem to come nearer!

There is little genuine pleasure in the ascent of the final few thousand feet of Kibo, and it is only when the edge of the crater has been attained that one appreciates all the pain as being worthwhile. The path which zigzags up the side of the mountain seems never-ending. The average walker begins by climbing perhaps 100 steps before resting, and this number of paces set by the individual becomes for a few hours the focal point of his existence. By the time 5,490 m (18,000 ft) is reached the distance covered between rests has been reduced to a few stumbling steps. The aim of the exercise is to reach the lowest part of the crater rim at 5,723 m (18,600 ft) which has been named Gillman's Point. After this some will continue onward to the highest point, but for most Gillman's will suffice. Halfway up the scree the initial determination to reach the top of Kilimanjaro has left the majority of people, and many retire back to the hut long before Gillman's has been gained. John Reader, in his book *Kilimanjaro*, puts the ascent of the scree into excellent perspective:

> Gillman's Point is 960 metres above Kibo Hut, that is almost the equivalent of three Empire State Buildings standing one on top of another. The horizontal distance between Kibo Hut and Gillman's Point is roughly 3,000 metres, so the gradient averages about 1:3.3 and the distance covered on the way up is about 3,300 metres—the equivalent of nine Empire State Buildings laid end to end up the incline. The climb is not difficult in mountaineering terms; you could say it is equivalent to scrambling up a staircase rather more than three kilometres long. Or you could say it is equivalent to clambering up the side of nine Empire State Buildings laid end to end at about sixteen degrees. But then at 4,710 metres, where the final ascent of Kilimanjaro begins, there is little more than half the density of oxygen which occurs on Manhattan or at the foot of most staircases. So, in effect, the aspiring climber attempts the equivalent of those feats with the equivalent of only one lung. The result is agonizing, there is no other word for it.[6]

On my first attempt I reached Gillman's Point and could go no further. I would like to think that my reason for failure was that I was only 15 years old, but it is more likely that Kilimanjaro was on that occasion simply too difficult for me. I returned the following year and this time reached the summit. Two items stand out clearly in my mind on this subsequent ascent. The first was that many of the names had changed; Bismark Hut had more appropriately become Mandara Hut, while Peter's Hut was now Horombo Hut. Kilimanjaro's summit had become Uhuru Peak (Freedom Peak) rather than Kaiser Wilhelm Spitze, probably better but there was something nice about KWS.

The second thing I remember was for me of far greater importance. During the ascent I developed a deep obsession about Mawenzi, little realising then that this battered old peak would be responsible for profoundly linking my life to mountains. There would be no escape from it. I knew I must climb it but this

[6] Reader, J.: *Kilimanjaro*; Elm Tree (London), 1982.

Ice sculpture in the Eastern Icefield.

presented problems for I would need to learn how to rock-climb. By joining the Mountain Club of Kenya I began this long process and after several years felt ready to attempt a "technical" mountain, and in April 1965 with two friends found myself once again at Marangu.

We followed the normal trail for two and a half days up to the edge of The Saddle, then branched off towards Mawenzi. A small hut is situated beneath the West Face at 4,600 m (15,093 ft) and we made this our base. It was the middle of the rainy season and the weather was bad, but during clear spells Kilimanjaro was more beautiful than I had ever seen it before. Both Kibo and Mawenzi were plastered with snow and it lay like a thick quilt across The Saddle. We had deliberately chosen April for several reasons, for we felt sure that Mawenzi had never been climbed at this time of year before. We could therefore legitimately regard our climb as a first "winter" ascent. The second reason was that Mawenzi's rock is notoriously bad and in the late afternoon the majority of routes to its summit are swept by rock-falls. Now the mountain was totally iced over and, although it would make the climb technically harder, it would be safer.

Our proposed route was that originally climbed by Oehler and Klute in 1912. The main feature of this is the Oehler Gully which is the most prominent feature up the steep West Face, and we were aware that two ice-falls in this gully would be the most difficult parts of the climb. The first stood at the foot of the face, while the second lay just beneath the summit itself. We spent an enjoyable day scouting the route to the start of the Oehler Gully, then at 4.00 am the following morning we set off on the main attempt. Shortly after daybreak I traversed to the base of the first ice-fall which rose above at an angle of approximately 60

Down Oehler Gully's snow-ice ramp, on Mawenzi's north-western flank.

degrees for 15 m (50 ft). The ice however was in excellent condition and it took me only 20 minutes to reach the top of the ice-fall. Now, with the confidence of knowing that the hardest section was beneath us, we moved quickly up the easier central section and, sharing leads, were soon working on the upper ice-fall. I had never seen such poor quality rock as that which graced the sides of the gully, and we climbed up the centre of the ice which at this point was some 25 m (80 ft) wide.

It was a cloudless day and the views down to The Saddle and across to Kibo were spectacular. By 1.00 pm we had gained the top of the Oehler Gully and were looking down the sheer 1,220-m (4,000-ft) East Face of Mawenzi. The summit, Hans Meyer Peak, stood over to our right, but we scaled two false summits before finally standing on the highest point of Mawenzi. It was a dream summit pinnacle with room on the top for only one person to stand, and although Kibo rose to the west over 600 m (2,000 ft) higher than us, we felt we were the conquerors of the entire mountain.

During the afternoon as we abseiled down the route I thought of how impressive the ascent of Mawenzi by Oehler and Klute in 1912 had been. At that time there could have been few more difficult mountains climbed in the European Alps. I also found myself thinking that as I had now successfully climbed both Kibo and Mawenzi there would be little to attract me back to Kilimanjaro, not realising that I was to make a further 17 ascents of Kibo. As we slid effortlessly down our ropes that afternoon in 1965 I was completely unaware that far across the mountain on the other side of Kibo, where the summit, Uhuru Peak, slopes away south-westward, it culminated in the largest mountain wall on the African continent—the Breach Wall. To its east the glaciers of the Heim, Kersten and Decken hung from the Southern Icefield like three giant, icy tentacles. By the mid-1960s each of these glaciers had been climbed once, although their general inaccessibility meant that little was known about them. This was truly Kilimanjaro's hidden secret and it would be 10 years before I would see it. Until then it could be reached only in dreams.

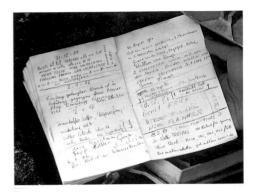

The pages of Mawenzi's summit notebook, bearing countless signatures, are steeped in climbing history.

It is 1912. An icy gale thrashes the flat, sandy surface of The Saddle, and the two men, both Germans, cower beneath the huge overhanging boulder, pulling their heavy tweed great-coats about them. Never for a moment during the long months of preparation for their small expedition to Kilimanjaro had they anticipated a storm of such intensity, and its suddenness and bite has now rendered them momentarily stunned. As they fight in vain to shield themselves from the fury of the storm which has crept up, catching them completely off guard, forcing them to take shelter beneath this massive rock jutting from the plain like an ungainly giant egg, the men are somehow contented, almost jubilant, and with good reason.

Oehler and Klute have now been on Kilimanjaro several weeks. It has not been easy for them. In fact never in all their years in the mountains have they experienced such cold, hardship and discomfort, but it has been profitable and certainly worth enduring because yesterday they became the first people to stand on the summit of Mawenzi.

At last the storm started to die as they thought back over the happenings of the previous two days. The great, friable, brown-coloured, pumice-like vertical wall above them. Impregnable. And then the breakthrough up the gully. Intricate ice-climbing. The crumbling rock which followed, and then the summit which turned out not to be the summit at all when the cloud cleared. Finally the indisputable highest point. The hasty descent and then the storm which pinned them to the side of the mountain for a long, cold night. The early morning start and the final descent to The Saddle, and then the advent of an even fiercer storm. This one, which had forced them to the flimsy protection of their present position.

Now the storm has completely dissolved. A sparkling patchwork has appeared in places in the sky, and the men, drenched and shivering, move from under the dripping rock. They start down the mountain away from the inhospitable barrenness of The Saddle, in the direction of their tent located at 3,960 m (13,000 ft) where there is vegetation at least.

A few weeks earlier Oehler and Klute and their small expedition had started up through the south-eastern forests from the little town of Marangu. They remembered how they had viewed the great white dome of Kibo with quiet disdain. True, it was the highest point of the mountain—Africa's roof—but it was a walk, and it had been climbed by two different parties who had returned with tales of the long hike up tortuous screes, followed by a walk round the crater rim to a summit which had turned out to be a dull, uninspiring plateau. This was not what Oehler and Klute had travelled all the way from Germany to climb; the real mountain, Mawenzi, lay to the east and that was where they headed.

The day after the storm was clear and sunny, as most are, and the mountaineers rested, basking in the sun by their tent. They had climbed Mawenzi more quickly than originally anticipated, food was still reasonably plentiful, and slowly their minds turned to the idea of climbing Kibo. Oehler had already climbed it in 1906, but had not reached the summit, and now it seemed fitting to him to crown their unquestionable achievement with a hike to the summit of the mountain. Klute, a glaciologist, was keen to explore the other side of Kilimanjaro, keeping beneath the 4,572-m (15,000-ft) level, and then climb up to the top from the west. They were about to make their first error of judgement on Kilimanjaro.

Three days later everything had gone according to plan. They were now north of Kibo and the weather was still holding. Here lay their major problem, for the weather was *too* good. There had been no protective cloud cover during their trek over the last three days, the sun had beaten down unmercifully, and they had traversed country more typical of the central Sahara than a 5,800-m (19,000-ft) peak. They had discovered no enticing oasis and, to add to their troubles, water rations had run out on the afternoon of the third day, just when they were beginning to realise that Kilimanjaro was much larger than they had thought. That night they decided to cut their losses and head for the summit from their present position. At least there would be ice higher on the mountain.

By early afternoon of their fourth day, Oehler and Klute had pulled themselves out of danger; they had reached the base of a relatively easy-angled glacier, their water supply was replenished and they settled down for the long night which would precede their climb up the glacier on the following morning.

The climb proved to be long and strenuous, but fortunately never technically difficult. By noon they had reached the crater rim and made the first ascent of what they named the Drygalski Glacier, after the polar explorer. They quickly crossed the crater floor and reached the summit in the early afternoon.

The two Germans had now been on Kilimanjaro for so long that their bodies were fully acclimatised. Dropping their ropes and climbing equipment near the summit, they moved down into a great chasm on the western side which they had noticed earlier that day. No sooner had they begun their descent than the first cloud they had seen in days began to swirl around the eerie amphitheatre in which they now found themselves. But still they continued to descend, scrambling down over steep, crumbling lava walls, and wishing at times they had brought their ropes. Soon visibility was reduced to only a few yards, but the going became easier. They had reached a steep scree slope which they were able to descend swiftly.

By late afternoon, totally lost but not worried, they decided to wait for the cloud to lift. They still had enough food for three days and melt-water was nearby. As the cloud started to lift the two men scrambled to the top of a rocky outcrop which would later be named the Shark's Tooth and, as they stared eastward through the rising mist, a view began to unfurl in front of them which left them stunned and motionless. Before them lay a near-vertical wonderland, a magnificent confusion of jumbled ice which rose for nearly a mile (one and a half kilometres) above them, shimmering in the last rays of the sun. They were the first recorded people to set eyes upon the south-western glaciers of Kibo. They had just descended for the first time what people would later call the Great Western Breach, and as they stood watching they realised that the other side of Kilimanjaro yielded a mountain wall of Himalayan proportions.

It is 1976. I am sitting on an icy ledge at 5,490 m (18,000 ft), two-thirds of the way up the Kersten Glacier—the steepest of the three major ice masses on the south-west side of Kibo. As I slip easily out of my dream, far beneath me, through swirling cloud I can see the Shark's Tooth, where Oehler and Klute first set eyes upon the face I am now climbing. Last night, Mark Savage and I slept at the base of the glacier and all day we have been climbing, weaving a new route up the Kersten's technically difficult cliffs. Oehler and Klute had been lucky. Everywhere they walked was untrodden ground; their adventure lay on an untouched mountain. For us today, to try to capture some of the pioneering atmosphere which came so easily to them, we must seek out difficult unclimbed passages like this long, steep ice-wall, a place where we can be sure nobody has ever been. Mark and I remained on "new" ground until we reached the summit

(*Opposite*) Giant groundsel frames the Breach Wall of Kibo. The icicle joining the Balletto Glacier with the Diamond Glacier above was climbed by Reinhold Messner on his first ascent of the Breach Wall in January 1978.

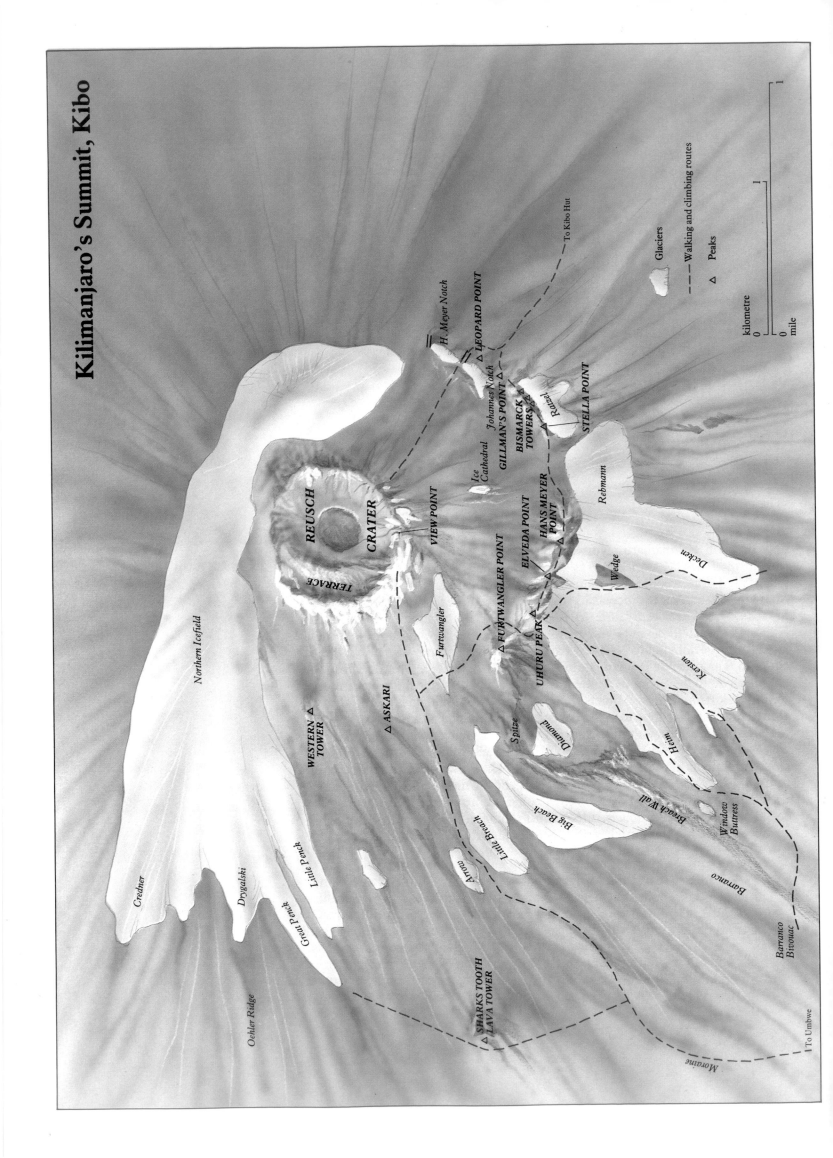

9 · The Forgotten Peak: Mount Meru

Iain Allan

The dark cone of Mount Meru rises to 4,600 m (14,978 ft) in northern Tanzania and stands imposingly above the town of Arusha. It is arguably the most elegant volcano in Africa but fails to secure a place amongst the greatest African peaks. Its height narrowly denies it a permanent snow-capped summit, and it is dwarfed by the magnitude of Kilimanjaro which stands only some 50 km (30 miles) to the east.

But Mount Meru *should* be recognised as a major mountain of Africa for there can be few peaks as pleasing to the eye. When viewed from the west, its graceful symmetry reaches skyward, casting a huge shadow across Maasailand, culminating in a stately summit pyramid of craggy cinder. From the east Meru appears as the giant volcano it is, with a caldera of spectacular proportion, a sheer-sided basin gradually descending to a point where no crater wall now exists. To the Maasai tribe who graze their cattle and goats beneath the western, northern and eastern slopes of the mountain, the name *Meru* means "that which does not make a noise", but in fact rumblings have been reported as recently as the early 1960s. The last eruption was probably in 1877, and lava rock or pyroclasts were blown out during October and December 1910.

It takes little knowledge of volcanoes to see that Meru fits the conventional shape more obviously than Mount Kenya, Elgon or Kilimanjaro's Mawenzi. The latter are silent and extinct, and look it. Meru emits an atmosphere of activity. It is a mountain on the move and probably once staged the grandest eruption and loudest bang ever seen or heard on the African continent.

Several million years ago the earth's crust was split open from the borders of Turkey to the mouth of the Zambezi River in Mozambique, and the Great Rift Valley was formed. Amidst this terrestrial confusion virtually all of East and Central Africa's volcanoes were formed. Mount Meru was no exception, and in its prime may have reached the height, or possibly even exceeded that of Kilimanjaro today. Geologists feel that Meru's crater, in all probability, once contained a large, very deep lake. They speculate that when the great ash-cone, which stands in the crater at the present time, was thrust up, the molten mass from the interior of the earth mingled with the water of the lake, which turned to steam. As a result one massive explosion rent the volcano apart and the entire eastern wall of the crater collapsed, the debris surging down the mountain slopes as a cascade of molten rocks and boiling mud. This avalanche was accompanied by a shower of ash and cinders which was deposited as a jumble of slag heaps, obliterating the countryside and blocking the rivers for many miles around the base of the mountain.

It is quite terrifying when one realises that all of this took place in, geologically speaking, comparatively recent times, and that probably thousands of animals, and possibly even people perished in the disaster.

Mount Meru.

(*Opposite*) Looking down over the ash-cone from the summit of Mount Meru to Kilimanjaro.

The vegetation of Mount Meru forms an island within an area of semi-arid grassland. It could be regarded as a microcosm of Kilimanjaro and this is not surprising when one considers that the 2,135-m (7,000-ft) contours of both mountains are only about 45 km (25 miles) apart. Meru rises from the plains abruptly, tapers steeply towards the summit, and its Alpine zone is very small.

The vegetation of the mountain is related to the age of the land surface, to the rivers, and to the altitude. It is at present undeveloped in relation to the land-form owing to repeated volcanic disturbances. The mountain is characterised by steep gorges, through which rivers run, and so the enclosing vegetation is hardly influenced by these water-courses. The terrain is precipitous and in an extremely unstable state. Up to an altitude of 2,440 m (8,000 ft), Mount Meru is thickly forested except for the dry northern slopes which are lightly wooded or semi-arid grassland. Above 2,500 m (8,200 ft) there is hagenia forest, secondary heath and tussock grassland. The Alpine zone above 3,660 m (12,000 ft) produces occasional plants but as it gains in height eventually becomes completely barren.

The lower rain forest of the mountain consists of a jumbled mass of juniper and *Podocarpus* trees. It is a very green, thick forest carpeted with ferns and nettles, while dripping lianes hang from the trees. Charming glades offer a sudden contrast to this intimidating region and make it possible for visitors to catch a glimpse of the mountain's wildlife. The Cape buffalo is the predominant mammal, but elephant, bushbuck, red forest duiker and black rhino are there too. The screeches of olive baboon (*Papio anubis*) frequently shatter the silence of this region, while Colobus monkeys swoop ghost-like from the forest canopy. I have spoken to someone who swears the elusive bongo exists in the Mount Meru rain forest but as far as I can discover this claim has never been substantiated.

Mount Meru's eroded walls are in stark contrast to the forest and grasslands on the lower slopes.

afternoon. It was a bleak shelter, with a floor formed of lava cinders, and everything was made worse by the fact that most of our party were tired and sick. We paid the price of a hasty ascent as mountain sickness firmly took its hold. I lay shivering in my flimsy sleeping bag through the long night, listening to the groans of my companions. I felt well, but there is nothing like hearing other people being sick to make one question one's own health, and it was with considerable relief when, at 3.00 am, I left the hut to attempt the summit with the remaining two healthy members of the group.

The huge screes on the western slopes of Mount Meru are formidable. They rise to the edge of the crater rim in one great grey sweep for nearly 923 m (3,000 ft), and I remember the pain of the ascent as excruciating. Time moved slowly and we never seemed to gain height. I tried to take my mind off the agony by counting the lights of Arusha which appeared from far below through the darkness like a distant, glowing triangle.

As the dawn broke my companions decided to return to the hut. Moving on alone I traversed away from the scree and made for easier-angled rock which seemed to lead more directly to the point I was making for. Scrambling up the rocks enabled me to gain altitude quickly and by 7.00 am I had reached the crater rim, only some 60 m (200 ft) north of the summit. The crater wall beneath me fell away vertically for nearly 1,220 m (4,000 ft), and I moved slowly along the rim to the summit.

It is one of the finest summits I have ever stood upon. Far below me, inside the main crater, I could see the ash-cone appearing through clouds. The morning was exhilaratingly clear and, as Kilimanjaro to the east shimmered regally, I could also see the elegant Longido Mountain to the north, and across westward to the Maasai plains and Monduli Mountain. After a delightful half hour on the summit, I started down towards the screes and the hut.

Porter and armed guard in the rain forest of Mount Meru.

In 1986, older, hopefully wiser, and with a deeper understanding of mountains, I returned to Mount Meru. During the years since I had first climbed it my thoughts had frequently returned to Tanzania's famous volcano. Was it really as difficult as I remembered it? Were the screes as tortuous as they now appeared in my memory? Or could the agony be attributed simply to the fact that it was my initiation to mountains? On many peaks since, whenever I have had to trudge up endless screes, images of Meru would often filter back into my mind. This journey back in time was for another reason as well. On countless occasions I had found myself nodding my head in agreement as other climbers extolled the wonders of the lower reaches of Mount Meru's slopes, whereas in reality I could remember nothing of this region. I felt it was time to go back and investigate.

Few parties now ascend the mountain from Olkokola. The entire massif is now encompassed within the Arusha National Park, and the most commonly used approach is from the eastern side. At the park headquarters the reaction of the rangers was one of shock when I informed them that I wished to climb the mountain alone, and I was pointedly told that the regulations did not allow for this. A guide was mandatory. This disappointed me greatly for the thought of spending several days alone on Meru appealed to me very much. A young man named Albano was hurriedly produced and, just as I was wondering of what earthly use he would be to me, a 1909 model Mauser rifle made in Argentina was thrust into his arms by a park official. This, I was told, would protect me from buffalo, of which there were many. The atmosphere was not conducive to debating the issue, and it was obvious to me that if I wished to climb Meru,

(*Following pages*) Mount Meru from the east.

Albano would be my companion. I was then informed that it would not be his job to assist me with my load. For this purpose I would require a porter and, before I could blink, Japheth was presented. I quickly reasoned that if one person must accompany me, two would make little difference, and several hours later, far from third-world bureaucracy, my small expedition finally began its trek towards Mount Meru.

Albano and Japheth were from the Warusha tribe who inhabit the country immediately south of the mountain, and both men turned out to be excellent companions. Physically they could not have been more opposite: Albano short and thickly set, while Japheth was tall and lithe. They shared two common traits: both were obviously very fit, and they possessed an endearing capacity for laughter. Their faces would explode into unabashed mirth at every opportunity, and I sensed immediately that not only would they perform their work competently, more important they would be fun to be with.

Our path led up through charming meadows and crossed many small streams. Signs of the presence of Cape buffalo were everywhere and from the way Albano moved, with his rifle at the ready, I could see that he was well aware of this. Later he would tell me how a friend of his, who was a ranger in the park, had been seriously gored by a buffalo several years before, whilst he was guiding a group of tourists towards the ash-cone in Mount Meru's crater.

Shortly after starting our morning hike a large female giraffe (*Giraffa camelopardalis*) followed by her baby of no more than two weeks old, had crashed from the thicket on our left and loped off ahead of us into the forest. Other crashing noises, this time more ominous, occasionally interrupted our pace throughout the morning, and we knew that buffalo grazed all around us.

As we approached the montane forest, yellow flowering *hypericums* appeared, surrounded by open patches of sedge grass upon which "red hot poker" lilies grew. Entering the forest we were in a world of green, shady glades. Spanish moss hung in great frizzled clumps from the juniper and *Podocarpus* trees, while the sudden red flash of the Hartlaub's turaco (*Turaco hartlaubi*) would frequently flit by into the depths of the trees.

We reached Merukama Hut, which stands at an altitude of 2,515 m (8,250 ft), shortly after midday, and were met by two friendly Warusha hut guards. The setting was idyllic despite the fresh elephant droppings strewn around the hut vicinity, and we were informed by the guards that a herd of about 20 elephants had been in this area for a week or so.

After lunch I decided to spend the afternoon reading, but distorted music pounded from the guard's battered radio, and my attempts to persuade them to turn down the volume proved futile. To find solitude, it would seem, even on the remoter peaks of East Africa, was rapidly becoming a task of major proportions. I therefore distanced myself from the hut, but upon my return several hours later the music continued as the men sat around engrossed in what would appear to be their major pastime—whittling away at large pieces of wood, forming them into giant spoons. I had seen this before during a trip to the Ruwenzori Mountains, where each afternoon the porters would devote several hours to spoon-making.

Modern East African popular music can be quite disturbing to Western ears. The beat, generally speaking, tends to be very monotonous and I have heard it described as "pulsating static". As it continued into the night I decided to sleep outside the hut, as far away as possible. The risk of elephants in the area was infinitely preferable to a long night subjected to this incessant drone, and I unrolled my sleeping bag beneath a large tree with strong branches conveniently positioned for a hasty ascent should the need arise. It turned out to be an uneventful night until about 3.00 am when it started to rain. I returned to the hut which by then was quiet, and slept soundly until 7.00 am.

Hagenia tree zone is situated in the afternoon cloud belt at 10,000 feet.

We left the hut soon after breakfast and continued up the muddy trail which was deeply rutted by Cape buffalo. Several different sightings were made of beautiful Colobus monkeys high above us, flitting from tree to tree. At approximately 2,750 m (9,000 ft), tall pencil cedar and East African olive trees grew thickly then gradually gave way to the hagenia region, the trees of which grow to massive sizes. Mountain swifts and pigeons flew overhead at incredible speeds, and in a distant clearing we were able to see the dark outlines of Cape Buffalo, justifying the name of the area—Tope La Mbogo, "Mud of Buffalo".

We were following a ridge which soon reached a gap in the vegetation and merged with the crater rim. This place which is known as Mgongo Wa Tembo, "The Elephant's Back", gave us our first good views of Mount Meru's crater. A sea of cloud boiled over the ash-cone, and the summit rose starkly above us on the other side of the crater. With the forest now behind us, we could look eastward to Kilimanjaro, which seemed to be in a state of eruption owing to the effects of a huge cumulus cloud bursting over its snowy summit like a billowing dragon.

The path led up through dense heather which grew some three metres (10 ft) in height, and eventually reached the saddle between the main peak and Little Meru—an outlying summit to the north. Here lay the remains of two huts which had been completely stripped by thieves some years previously, and I was glad that I had brought my small tent to this point. At 3,570 m (11,700 ft) it was going to be a chilly night.

In the afternoon Albano and I scrambled up to the crater rim which was about 30 minutes walk from the saddle. It was a spectacular view, as splendid as any I have seen in the mountains of East Africa and, despite a cold wind which blew from the north-west, we sat for some time watching clouds sizzle below in the main crater. Albano told me of how once every year the Warusha enter the crater from the east and offer a sacrifice of one cow or ram in order to pray for rain. He went on to explain that a selected group of 12 persons, led by one small girl and one small boy, pray for the rain. By Presidential decree these worshippers are given free passage into the National Park, and must be met with no hindrance whatsoever. The ritual has been going on for countless generations, and Albano was adamant that it always rains within two days of the prayers.

It was a windy, cold night and I was eager to begin climbing at 4.00 am next morning. Albano and Japheth decided to stay at the camp in the saddle, and I was secretly pleased that I would be going alone to the summit just as I had done over 20 years earlier. There was little vegetation now and I was in a dark world

Mount Meru emerges from a blanket of cloud.

Clive Ward's Brochen Spectre near the summit of Mount Meru.

of grey cinders, following an indistinct path which wound its way closely to the edge of the crater. My route was totally exposed to the wind which was now, if anything, more violent, and ferocious dust-devils were whipped up around me. Slate-grey volcanic dust blasted into my face, and the scree was frustrating—two steps up, then one down!

After several hours I reached a small col below a jagged outcrop of shattered basalt, and estimated that I was now only about half an hour from the summit. As daylight broke, the wind began to settle. I could now look clearly down into the ash-cone, and it was not long before I had gained the point below the summit from where I had seen the crater during my first ascent. Memories came flooding back and in a calm, clear morning like the one so long ago, I found myself standing on Meru's summit once again.

There was no reason for haste and I idled in the sun for about an hour. The route from the east had been considerably easier than the one I remembered from the west and, as I intended to descend only as far as my camp, I had plenty of time on my hands. I gazed down the sheer 1,220-m (4,000-ft) precipice into the crater and wondered at the possibilities of scaling this face on some future expedition, but it did not appear attractive, as it seemed to be very shattered with a pumice-like texture.

Eventually I pulled myself away and slowly hiked down the path. Cloud now enveloped me and, against the sun, it suddenly bathed me in a Brochen Spectre, where I could see my shadow greatly exaggerated, encircled by the colours of the rainbow, hovering out over the crater. It was one of the most perfect I had ever seen, and as I speeded down the path to where I could see Albano waiting, my shadow danced elusively in the clouds beside me.